ISSUES IN EUROPEAN BUSINESS

Peter Lawrence

MACMILLAN
Business

First published 1998 by
MACMILLAN PRESS LTD
Houndmills, Basingstoke, Hampshire RG21 6XS
and London
Companies and representatives
throughout the world

ISBN 0–333–68933–X hardcover
ISBN 0–333–68934–8 paperback

A catalogue record for this book is available
from the British Library.

This book is printed on paper suitable for recycling and made from
fully managed and sustained forest sources.

10   9   8   7   6   5   4   3   2   1
07   06   05   04   03   02   01   00   99   98

Printed and bound in Great Britain by
Antony Rowe Ltd
Chippenham, Wiltshire

To my students
at Loughborough University Business School

'If you want clarity you cannot have faith,
if you want truth you cannot have clarity.'

Søren Kirkegaard

Contents

Acknowledgements

This book draws on a number of research projects on which I have worked during the 1990s. First and foremost, I am a founder member of a multicountry research group known to its members as MODEM (Managers on Developing European Markets), formed in 1989. This group has been inspired and coordinated by academics from the Département de Politique Générale de l'Entreprise at ESC Lyon in Eastern France. The MODEM group carried out a study of executive's perceptions of the Single European Market, and later a study of the determinants of strategy among European companies. This second study was funded by the European Union. I have benefited greatly from involvement in these multicountry projects, and in particular from the quality of intellectual leadership offered by the French, who masterminded the research.

Since 1994 I have been a visiting professor at Nene College of Higher Education in Northampton. In this context I have been part of an ongoing study of the experiences of newly internationalising companies, a project I have worked on with Valerie Anderson, Stuart Graham and Kevin Lamb of Nene College, and more recently with Grahame Boocock, my colleague at the Loughborough University Business School. Nene College funded this project.

Also at Nene College, together with my friend Barbara Senior, I have carried out a questionnaire survey of the values and attitudes of managers from a variety of European and non-European countries. The data analysis was completed just in time to enable me to draw on some of the findings in Chapters 10 and 11. This project too was funded by Nene College.

I would like to thank my MODEM colleague Murray Steele of the Cranfield School of Management for permission to use his case study on the European brewing industry. I would also like to thank my friend Vincent Edwards at Buckinghamshire College of Higher Education for permission to quote from his book *Hungary since Communism* (Macmillan, 1997), and from the Proceedings of the various CREEB (Centre for Research on Eastern European Business) conferences that he organised at Buckinghamshire College.

Some of the ideas in Chapter 10 I was able to 'test run' in my inaugural lecture at Loughborough University Business School in February 1997, and was most heartened by the flattering things that people said at the time!

Finally I would like to thank Freda Clarke, my secretary at Loughborough University Business School, for a fast and friendly preparation of the manuscript and for cheerfully carrying out all sorts of assignments that have facilitated the work.

PETER LAWRENCE

CHAPTER 1

A thin red line

The theme of the present book is the tension between the diversity of Europe and the forces for homogenisation. The different chapters or groups of chapters treat different business and management issues in Europe, but they all touch on this central question of diversity versus homogeneity.

It may be helpful to signpost this enterprise. To start with we would claim that the problem this book addresses, the tension between diversity and homogenising forces, is a real one, and this is true in several ways. First of all Europe is diverse. A rather large member of separate, independent countries are packed into a modest space. These countries have different histories and cultures, and mostly different languages. And for hundreds of years these countries were rent by war.

Secondly, not only is Europe diverse, but this diversity tends to differentiate it – not absolutely but relatively. That is to say, some other areas of the world are made up of groups of independent countries that have much more in common with each other than do the countries of Europe. The Arabic-speaking Muslim countries of the Middle East or the Spanish-speaking Catholic countries of South America are clearly less heterogeneous than Europe. Likewise if one compares Europe, or at least Western Europe, with other members of the famous triad – Japan and the USA – then Europe is clearly the only one that is:

- made up of a lot of different countries,
- marked by linguistic, cultural and institutional variety.

As a counterpoint to the diversity of Europe, which we are viewing here as a differentiating feature, the Japanese like to claim homogeneity as a defining characteristic.

Thirdly, if one takes a medium-term geopolitical view that European diversity is diminishing, or at least that there are forces for concentration, for a greater investment of energy and attention on Europe, then consider the following:

- There have been no real wars in Europe since 1945, though violence has occurred in the 1990s attendant on the break-up of the former USSR and Yugoslavia.
- France and Germany, the historic enemies, have been reconciled.
- The European countries have given up most of their former colonies, which in turn has given them a more European focus, especially in trade matters.
- The rival communist system has disappeared, and Germany has been reunified.

On top of all this the European Union (EU) has grown from a six-country block in 1958 to a fifteen-country block in 1995, with other European states having associate membership while former communist countries clamour to get in. The EU has put through its programme of non-tariff barrier abolition and the Single European Market initiative, and it aspires to monetary union – and more besides.

But the forces for homogenisation are not only geopolitical. They also reside in the internationalisation of business. A whole range of factors – speed of communication, the IT revolution, the ease of cross-border fund transfer and cross-border financing, the greater ease with which design and manufacture can be integrated cross-border, the enhanced possibilities of organising and controlling off-shore manufacture, the growing acceptability of cross-border acquisition and merger activity, the rise of cross-border joint ventures and strategic alliances, and more besides – have all made business much more international at the end of the twentieth century than it was a mere twenty years earlier. And running through all this is ever increasing competition, leading to concentration and increasing company size, a need by the larger players to compete in many country markets, and certainly to have a presence in the three parts of the triad – Japan, the USA and Europe. Customer expectations rise with enhanced competition, leading to greater research and development (R&D) costs, larger marketing expenditure, shorter product life cycles and downward pressure on costs. This in turn fuels the drive to increase sales, enter new markets and develop sales abroad, thus allowing larger-scale manufacturing operations, lower unit costs, economies of scale and scope, and more chance to amortise R&D and marketing costs.

Now all these developments have 'a life of their own', are independent of the particular countries in which firms operate or are headquartered. If one asks executives from different European countries about what they see as business trends in the 1990s, as in the multicountry study reported in Chapter 2, there is a surprising cross-country consistency about their answers. They refer to Europeanisation and internationalisation, to greater competition and its manifestations noted above, to industry concentration and the progressive elimination of medium-sized players, to the growing importance of segmentation, where a segment is a subset of product markets, and so on. And all this is independent of the policies and purposes of the EU, but has been enhanced and facilitated by the EU and in particular by its Single European Market programme, outlined in Chapter 2.

The homogenisation forces show up in yet another way. If one takes executives from the same industry in different European countries, as in the multicountry study described in Chapter 4, then again their perceptions of industry developments, the way their industry is segmented and the overall strategic frame of reference for their companies are remarkably similar. The evidence seems to be that one can take any industry and identify operational and strategic commonalties across country borders. But this is not the whole story: there is also natural and persistent diversity.

Indeed in this context one can repeat the procedure just described. One can take a single industry and examine it in a variety of national European settings, checking things such as variations in consumer taste, packaging conventions, productivity levels, degree of industry concentration, cross-border ownership stakes, export capability, import substitution measures, generation of employment and contribution to the national economy. We have done this with the brewing industry in Chapter 3, and are able to demonstrate a massive range of country-to-country differences, and even some unprogrammed country-specific behaviours including the impact of pubs on partner selection and the propensity to engage in smuggling!

There is of course an arbitrary element in all this. Since the world is divided into different countries – sovereign states – then every entrepreneur must be a citizen of somewhere, every company that is founded belongs to one country rather than another. So at the outset every company is surrounded by a national culture, a regulatory presence and a market bounded by national borders, however fluid. All this may impact upon and shape the development of companies and industries in any given country. To stay with the example of brewing, consider that if Freddy Heineken had been born German rather than Dutch he would have brewed beer according to the 1516 purity laws, sold it primarily within a 50 kilometre radius of the brewery, and Heineken would not have become the world's third biggest brewery.

Or again, while there are underlying business trends and perceptible determinants of corporate strategy, in combination these do not cause all companies in the same industry, or all companies in the same country, to behave in the same way. But there are various planks in the argument concerning the ability of companies to sustain difference.

The first point is introductory, and this is that the literature distinguishes between global industries and multidomestic ones. Companies in global industries have largely standardised products, which they sell in a variety of national markets to exploit economies of scale and scope. The first priority is global integration, in the sense of technically efficient production and logistically efficient sourcing and distribution. Japanese consumer electronics companies are often cited as examples of companies operating in a characteristically global industry. A multidomestic industry, on the other hand, is one that recognises the need to adapt products and services to suit different national markets. Local responsiveness is the key requirement for companies operating in multidomestic industries. Detergents for household washing, some food processing and personal care products are often cited as multi-domestic industries. Interesting for our purposes is the tendency in the literature for Europe to be associated with the notion of multidomestic industry, a tacit tribute to European diversity.

Secondly, a mid 1990s study of four industries in several EU countries suggested that companies in these industries were subject to demands for both global integration and local responsiveness, without either of these pressures becoming dominant and leading to global or multidomestic industry status; more properly, companies in these industries should be classified as 'mixed', and therefore having a greater range of operating behaviours and strategic choices (Atamer, 1996), a more subtle tribute to European diversity.

Thirdly, the same study confirmed the contention in the relevant literature to the effect that the main cause of transition to global industry status is the presence of mounting R&D costs. The idea is that these costs can only be amortised by volume manufacture and sales, enabling economies of scale. At the same time the study identified a number of other determinants that serve to place companies on the global versus multidomestic axis. The more determinants there are of a phenomenon, the more varied will be the range of outcomes.

Fourthly, the study showed that companies in the same industry might have a number of different 'logics of internationalisation'. That is to say, all the companies in the industry might engage in international activity, and manufacture and sell in a variety of countries (in this case European countries), but this international activity will have different strategic rationalisations.

Finally, the study suggested that companies in the same industry might react differently to business development and strategic constraints. Some, probably most, would recognise the constraints and 'play by the rules'. But a few would seek to reconfigure the constraints and develop more independent international strategies.

These particular ideas are explored in more detail in Chapter 5, but have been reviewed briefly at this stage because they add a strategic dimension to the case for European diversity. That diversity is highlighted in another quite different way. That is, most of the discussion of companies adapting to foreign markets and international exigencies focuses, quite understandably, on larger companies that are already established players in the international scene. But part of the staggering growth in world trade that has occurred in the last two decades of the twentieth century has been the result of mostly smaller companies engaging for the first time in international activity – exporting, cross-border merger or acquisitions, setting up in greenfield manufacturing sites in other countries and so on. In recognition of this, Chapter 6 is devoted to a discussion of the experiences of a sample of British companies newly engaging in international operations in the 1990s. Not to prefigure this later discussion, the simple point to be made at this stage is that internationalisation is a challenge in that it poses problems and contingencies precisely because of the differences between countries. What is more, in the study cited above the British companies encountered more problems in their ventures in other European countries than further afield in Asia or North America.

At the start of this chapter we suggested that the EU is clearly a homogenising force. The EU's principal achievement, however, has been to address the issue of tariff and regulatory differences between the member countries. The EU has not, however, addressed the matter of cultural differences between these countries. These cultural and perhaps even more importantly institutional differences continue to shape business systems and management values. Chapter 10 briefly reviews the evidence for such differences over the last quarter century. It is interesting to note that a late 1990s survey of management values and beliefs, conducted by the author and others, has confirmed a number of the differences between managers in the targeted European countries that were demonstrated in classic studies in the 1970s and 1980s. The principal unifying feature revealed in the study is a near universal recognition of heightened competition translating into pressure, change and insecurity for individual managers.

Finally, the transformation of Eastern Europe is among the business issues discussed in this work. This discussion is for the most part intrinsic in the sense of trying to present a before and after picture, of trying to identify developments and make sense of what is happening. At the same time the collapse of European communism beautifully highlights the tension between diversity and conformity.

At first sight, of course, the fall of European communism represented a substantial move towards homogeneity. From the end of the Second World War until 1989–91 Central and Eastern Europe had a different ideology, a different political system, a different and largely closed off economic system and a trading bloc (COMECON) that was counterpoised to the EU in the West. All this was swept away, with the former communist states aspiring to be democratic, capitalist and rich – as they perceived the West to be. The biggest divide in Europe since the Reformation had gone.

But with the benefit of hindsight we can now see that the force of communism masked a greater range of differences between the countries. Most obviously communism suppressed ethnic differences, which reemerged with disastrous consequences in Yugoslavia and the former USSR, and also broke up Czechoslovakia, albeit peacefully. With the benefit of hindsight we can now see that these countries did have different experiences under communism, did develop in different ways. So that in their different ways Poland and Hungary liberalised before the other states, the COMECON countries had different sized private sectors, different trading patterns within COMECON and so on.

What is more the economic experiences of these countries in the post-communist period have differed. The immediate effect of the fall of communism was to plunge the region into GDP shrinkage (their economies actually contracted), but the more successful (or fortunate) countries have emerged from this phase, albeit at different times – Poland in 1992, Slovenia in 1993 and the Czech Republic, Hungary and Slovakia in 1994 (EBRD, 1996)

But there are more sensational differences. Albania has lost 10 per cent of its population as a result of emigration (mostly to Greece); Bulgaria offers an average industrial wage that is on a par with that of Egypt; the Czech Republic has unemployment rates that are not only low for the region but would also be enviable in France or Spain; Hungary has been terrifically successful in attracting FDI (foreign direct investment) – 20 of the world's largest 35 companies now operate in Hungary – and so on.

There is probably something else at stake here. It may be too soon to say, but what we are seeing in the countries of Eastern Europe is arguably not only different rates of progress of down the road of capitalist transformation, but also variations on the themes of both capitalism and transformation. After all there are differences between the forms of capitalism in Western Europe, between say Britain and Germany, or France and Sweden, and it is likely that these differences will also arise in Eastern Europe.

Hence the present book discusses a number of themes in European business both substantively, for their own sake, and in relation to the overall idea of the tension between diversity and homogenisation. With regard to the overall idea, our purpose is to explore various dimensions rather than to pronounce judgement and give Europe a score of seven out of ten or whatever for advancing homogeneity! Indeed there seem to be so many trends and counterforces, so many spheres and levels of analysis, such various manifestations, that an intellectual mapping of the territory is likely to do more to advance our understanding than would some attempt to pronounce a finite judgement.

References

Atamer, T (1996) 'The Dynamics of competition in Europe: Top Managers Cognitions in Mixed Industries', final report to EU on contract CHRXCT 93-02-93.

European Bank for Reconstruction and Development (EBRD) (1996) *Transition Report*, London: EBRD.

1992 and all that

After years when nothing very exciting seemed to happen in the organisation that was popularly known as the Common Market and is now officially known as the European Union (EU), a resolution emerged in the middle of the 1980s to realise the original intention of the founders of the Common Market: to turn it into a real market entity with no internal barriers to the exchange of goods and services. This objective became enshrined in the Single European Act of 1986.

According to this Act the Common Market was to be transformed into a Single European Market (SEM), or in American, into a 'unified market', by the eliminating of non-tariff barriers, actual tariffs themselves having been eliminated in the early years of the Common Market, that is, to say, in or after 1958. But what were these non-tariff barriers? The answer is to indicate a variety of constraints operated within the Community, of which the most important were:

- Different technical and safety requirements, requiring products to be separately certified within the different countries of the Community.
- Restrictions on the free flow of capital and Constraints on the cross-border provision of financial services.
- Border controls and the associated documentation, which had slowed down the trans-shipment of goods and raised the price of that operation.
- An absence of rules for public procurement, requiring member governments and other public authorities to encourage suppliers in other member states to tender for contracts.
- Lack of harmonisation of (professional) qualifications by means of mutual recognition.

The idea was that the deliberative committee work and enabling legislation should be finalised by the end of 1992 so that the SEM would be come a reality on I January 1993. The time keeping was not perfect, but most of the work got done. The questions to be addressed in this chapter are as follows:

- Did it matter, did it make a difference?
- How was the SEM appraised and understood by industrialists and executives (as opposed to economists and Eurocrats)?
- How did these industrialists and executives put the SEM into context, that is, with what trends and developments did they associate it?

Anticipating the Single European Market

The build-up to the SEM generated a lot of interest and discussion. Enthusiasm for the single market was varied between the EU member countries, with an early survey (Ackermann, 1988) showing France to be the most enthusiastic, and Germany the least inclined among the surveyed countries to see 1992 as a landmark. Nonetheless the overall level of interest was high, notwithstanding the fact that the coming of the SEM had to share the limelight with the fall of European communism (see later chapters).

The approaching SEM also generated a substantial body of literature, or rather three overlapping bodies of literature. The first of these was the work of economists: largely deductive discussion, making predictions in terms of the laws of economics. This literature deals in rational inference; it is impersonal and verges on the economistic.

The second body of literature may best be labelled 'Eurocratic'. It was Brussels based, or at least Brussels inspired and represented 'the official view' of the then European Community (EC). It very cogently put the case for the SEM and the elimination of all non-tariff barriers and underlined the wastefulness and limitations of the pre-1992 state of affairs. But this Eurocratic literature went beyond a justification of EC policy to forecast the range of desirable consequences that should result from implementaction of the SEM. This literature reached its high point in what became known as the Cecchini Report (Cecchini, 1988), which committed itself to some quite precise predictions, including:

- 4.5 per cent growth in the EC GDP,
- a simultaneous cooling of the economy as a result of a 6.1 per cent drop in consumer prices,
- an average improvement in the public finances of the EC to the tune of 2.2 per cent of GDP,
- a boost to employment within the Community, with 1.8 million new jobs being created and a reduction of around 1.5 per cent in the prevailing unemployment rate.

It is worth pausing to note just how remarkable and remarkably confident these claims were – they went beyond what political party leaders typically promise in the euphoria of a general election!

The third body of literature was the work of academics and consultants and was aimed at practitioners – executives and companies – telling them what to do to make the most of the opportunities that would be presented by the SEM. This literature also tended to be very positive, urging that:

- 1992 would be jolly important!
- It would change everything.
- It represented a big opportunity for farsighted, strategically aware companies.

As James Dudley, the author of one of the most successful books of the genre put it:

> The Single European Act heralds a new era of economic and political opportunity. An environment will be created that which fosters wealth and job creation across the whole of the Economic Community (Dudley, 1989, p. 17).

Rather less prominent in the 1992 literature were discussions that took the views of executives and industrialists as the *point de départ*, rather than those of economists, Eurocrats and consultants, who in their various ways were all selling something *to* industry. Indeed there seems to have been only one serious piece of research on the perceptions and expectations of company executives, a study carried out in four industries across seven EC member countries, organised by a leading French business school, ESC Lyon. This study has a much wider interest in that it sought to contextualise executives' understanding of the SEM as well as to relativise it, with the result that the study is very illuminative of trends and developments in European business at the start of the decade.

This Lyon-based research group took the title MODEM (Managers on Developing European Markets) and published its 'hot off the press' findings before the official inception of the SEM (Calori and Lawrence, 1991). Because of the wide-ranging nature of this study – executives were asked about developments in their industries, in their companies and among their competitors *before* being quizzed on their perception of the SEM – it is a good introduction to some of the business concerns of the last decade of the century.

An executive view

The MODEM study took four industries and studied them in depth by means of interviews with senior executives. The industries were brewing, motor cars, retail banking and book publishing, and the study covered seven of the then twelve member countries of the Community, *viz.* Britain France, Germany,

Italy, Spain, Denmark and Holland, that is, all of the larger EC countries and some of the smaller ones. The idea was to identify several leading companies in each of the four industries in each of the seven countries, and to seek interviews with executives who were senior enough to have an overall view and a responsibility for future development. This framework yielded a sample of nearly one hundred companies and a slightly larger interview sample in that more than one executive was interviewed at some of the companies. Throughout the emphasis was not on collecting data external to the companies but on understanding the purposes and perceptions of senior mangers, the situation of their companies and the expected impact of the SEM.

Segmentation and Europeanisation

Many of the interviewees in the MODEM study emphasised the importance of segmentation, where a segment is a subset of products and/or markets within an industry. This testimony occurred across all four of the industries studied.

What the executives were saying was that the notion of 'an industry', as in 'the car industry' or 'the pharmaceuticals industry', is too crude, fails to differentiate and imposes a spurious uniformity. Industries, in fact, are often made up of different product-market subsets, that is, they are agglomerations of segments. Knowing this, however, will not necessarily enable the outsider to know what the segments are in any particular case. Consider the publishing industry. Whenever I question students they always reply that the segments are:

- Hardback versus paperback.
- Fiction versus non-fiction.

Perfectly sensible of course, but not what the MODEM interviewees said. Their segmentation was along the following lines:

- General literature, that is all fiction – hardback and paperback – including youth fiction and children's literature.
- 'Heavy' books, that is, art books, encyclopaedias, reference books, other big books.
- Academic and scientific.
- School books.

With retail banking the segments will include:

- Accounts (money transmission) for low-to medium-waged or salaried customers.

- Accounts, loans and advice for small business proprietors, shopkeepers and sole traders.
- HNWIs (high net worth individuals), that is rich people, whether as a result of their income, assets or both.
- Direct banking (telephone banking).
- Investment funds.

So the first consideration is to note that although the layman's notion of 'the industry' does have significance for insiders and practitioners, it is regarded as inadequately expressing the variable dynamics that are at work. The second issue is that of understanding why this is so, and this is probably a reflection of the market maturity of Europe. When products are new and markets unsatisfied, the demand is simply for some and then for more. When prohibition ended, people just wanted liquor, irrespective of type. But three quarters of a century later it is possible to point to segments in brewing:

- Low alcohol or non-alcoholic beers.
- Ordinary beers.
- Premium or strong beers.
- Speciality beers, such as aperitif beers or beers for special occasions.

In short, wealth is not the same as maturity. Some Asian countries may well be closing the wealth/disposable income gap with Western Europe but they are still not mature markets in the European sense, and segmentation is not as important.

The third issue is the recognition that in Europe these segments have different dynamics: supply and demand, satisfaction of need, the maintenance of competitive advantage and operational contingencies may all vary from segment to segment within the same industry. Hence it is increasingly meaningless to speak of a company's strategy in a given industry, where the emphasis is rather on strategies for discrete segments.

Fourth, business opportunities will increasingly be defined in terms of segments. The argument is easy to grasp if one looks at new markets, most obviously those in Eastern Europe. For motor manufacturers the luxury car segment scarcely exists in post-communist Eastern Europe, but the economy family car segment is of considerable importance.

Finally the segments are susceptible to differing degrees of Europeanisation or even internationalisation. Take the motor industry again. It is the luxury car segment that is most international – Porsche, Jaguar and Mercedes sell worldwide. Or consider the publishing industry, where different segments display marked contrasts in relation to internationalisation. The academic–scientific segment has world-wide potential: a university-based professional readership will demand the same works, and probably study them in the same language – English. In the MODEM sample of publishing companies, the Dutch company Elsevier was proud to be a major player in the academic–scientific segment, and had actually ceased to publish anything in Dutch. At the other extreme the school book segment is heavily tied to the particular country's education system. For example in Britain the critical developments impacting on the school book segment were, first, LMS (local management of schools) in the 1980s – the delegation to school (governor) level of budgetary responsibility and therefore the possibility of choosing between spending options (books or laboratory equipment, playing fields or school drama); and second the national syllabus in the 1990s, requiring a new generation of textbooks. Not much scope for Europeanisation here.

Bipolarisation

The MODEM study also highlighted a trend towards bipolarisation, in the sense of companies moving towards being big players in a number of segments simultaneously or concentrating on servicing a single segment/niche or just one or two niches. The idea is that this bipolarising trend is being driven both by the rise of technological and marketing developments and by the tendency for stronger segmentation noted in the previous section. The consequence of the bipolarisation trend is progressive elimination of the middle ground, of medium-sized generalist (multisegment) companies, as they downsize and specialise in niches or upsize to compete effectively in most of the industry's segments.

This trend was apparent in all four industries in the study, albeit more in some than in others. Representatives of several of the publishers spoke of getting into the big league, becoming global players, as well as fall-out in the industry and so on, while at the same time one could point to the emergence of companies specialising in a particular segment. Elsevier is again a case in point, with a senior executive speaking in 1990 of the company withdrawing from general publishing in the Netherlands (and in the Dutch language) in order to concentrate on the English-language scientific books segment (see previous section) on a worldwide front. Interestingly this executive observed that in the first few years in which the company pursued this policy, sales did not increase but margins tripled!

The same phenomenon was observable in the brewing industry. Large brewers with multiple products and strong brands selling in a variety of countries were coexisting with small brewers producing premium or specialist products for niche markets – with increasingly fewer medium-sized brewers in between. Perhaps the most interesting case was that of the Dutch brewer Grolsch. At the time this company was virtually a one-product brewer offering a very nice premium lager, usually sold in attractive swing-top bottles. Grolsch is located in the town of Enschede in the eastern part of the Netherlands, very close to the German border. A local *bon mot* was that this area of the Netherlands was the most egalitarian because everyone could drink Grolsch, whereas in the big towns of the west – Amsterdam, Utrecht and so on – Grolsch was only for the privileged! This idea was captured in a successful advertising slogan, which showed a beautifully chilled, tantalising bottle of Grolsch above the slogan 'Een dagje drink je geen bier meer, maar drink je even Grolsch' (one day you'll stop drinking beer, and just drink Grolsch). The interesting thing is that Grolsch exported a large proportion of its produce; that is, Grolsch is a premium product filling an old-fashioned quality niche in several countries.

It seems that the SEM is impacting on this bipolarisation trend by removing non-tariff barriers and thus making it easier for big players to rationalise and increase the scale of their operations, and for niche players to serve the same niche in many countries rather than simply in their domestic market.

The same development was anticipated rather than observed in retail banking, with representatives of this industry speaking of a 'shake out' that could produce a smaller number of very big banks doing everything (operating in all segments). But at the same time these spokesmen envisaged particular niches such as small businesses or wealthy individuals increasingly being catered for by specialist banks. Once again the SEM, with its planned liberalisation of financial service markets, is facilitating this trend, particularly in the form of the specialist institution servicing the same niche in several countries.

In the motor industry bipolarisation is a fact rather than a trend. In Europe six companies are clearly recognised as generalists in the sense of making a *range* of cars of different sizes and prices, rather than specialising in vehicles at one or other end (segment) of the market. Leaving out the Japanese manufacturers, who have set up operations in Britain alone, these six are Ford, General Motors (Opel and Vauxhall), Fiat, Peugeot (including Citroën), Renault and VAG (Volkswagen and Audi). Another group of manufacturers are operating within one or two price–quality–performance segments at the top end of the market only (Porsche, Jaguar, Mercedes and BMW), and doing so in many countries on the basis of a quite small vehicle per year output.

At the start of the 1990s the new trend in this industry was a blurring of this generalist versus specialist distinction, with generalists taking over specialists, *viz.* Jaguar by Ford, Masserati, Ferrari and Alfa Romero by Fiat and Saab by General Motors. The dividing line was also blurred for a while by the strategic alliance between generalist Renault and semispecialist Volvo, though this did not last. The critical issue here will be whether the up-market specialists will be given enough real and apparent independence by their masters to continue to enjoy credibility in their segments. The evidence so far suggests that this will be the case, though there was a nasty moment in the mid 1990s when Ford threatened to make Jaguar cars in Detroit City.

Concentration

Concentration refers to the domination of particular industries by a small number of big players, that is, to the situation where one or two companies between them have a large market share and account for a high proportion of the output. Within the EU concentration is a trend rather than an achieved state. It is a trend in the sense that:

- there was a lot of concentration in the 1980s,
- The executives in the MODEM study interviewed in 1990 were confident that this trend would continue in the 1990s, and
- on the whole that view has been justified.

Concentration was a feature of all the industries in the study, though in varying degrees. The previous section referred to some spectacular takeovers in the car industry, but perhaps less publicised developments in banking offer the strongest example. Consider for instance Denmark. In the late 1980s two superbanks, Den Danske Bank and Unibank, emerged as a result of a wave of mergers, as follows:

Den Danske Bank, Denmark's largest bank
Handelsbanken, Denmark's second largest bank   } Den Danske Bank
Den Danske Provinz Bank, Denmark's sixth largest bank

SDS, Denmark's third largest bank
Privat Banken, Denmark's fourth largest bank   } Unibank
Andels Banken, Denmark's seventh largest bank

These two merged entities are reckoned to have had 55 per cent of the Danish retail banking business by the start of the 1990s. A similar development occurred in Spain in 1990–91 when Banco Bilbao and Banco Vizcaya merged to become Banco Bilbao Vizcaya, and Banco Hispano-Americano and Banco Central became Banco Central Hispano Americano. This trend towards concentration in Spanish banking continued into the 1990s.

In the Netherlands the country's two most prominent banks, AMRO and the ABN, merged in 1990. The MNB took over the Postbank from the Dutch post office and later took over what was left of Barings after its collapse and is now known as the ING Bank. This was seen as remarkable by the Dutch people since the old MNB had a rather homely image as the traditional bank for self-employed craftsmen, shopkeepers, and small businesses. It used to be known affectionately as 'de bank voor de slaager om de hoek', the bank for the butcher's shop round the corner.

In Britain, albeit subsequent to the study reported here, one of the Big Four, banks, the Midland, was acquired by the Hong Kong and Shanghai Bank, and in 1996 another of the Big Four, Lloyds, bought the TSB.

So far, then, we have argued that concentration is a trend, and it was perceived as such, albeit in differing degrees by the industries studied. But there are some qualifications and distinctions to be made.

First of all, if we hold the industry constant the same industry may exhibit different degrees of concentration in the different EU countries. In publishing for example there were some 15 big players at the time of the study – Mondadori, Pearson, Reed, Hachette, Bertelsmann and so on – offering a high degree of concentration in some countries such as the UK and Germany but not in others. One of the Spanish executives commented: 'The Spanish market is very much fragmented. Last year [1989] 44000 books were published by 250 publishers'. There is also the paradox of Denmark. The Danish population is a mere five million (outnumbered by the population of pigs) and there is 22 per cent VAT on books, yet the country is served by numerous publishers and the number of new titles per year per 1000 of population is ten times higher than in the USA.

Likewise the brewing industry is highly concentrated in Holland and Denmark due to the dominance of Heineken (70 per cent of the market) and Carlsberg (80 per cent of the market) respectively, but much less concentrated in the UK, where at the time of the research some 80 per cent of the market was served not by the top brewer but by the top six. And in Germany at that time the top five brewers had only 12 per cent of the market, although some concentration has since taken place.

So concentration is a trend, but it varies between industries and between countries. We may also distinguish between concentration at the national level (the market share of the top one or two companies in any given country) and concentration at the European or at least EU level. At the European level, statistics in the form of agglomerations of market shares are less reliable, but with this qualification the market share in Europe of the top four companies seems to range from around 10 per cent for retail banking to some 50 per cent for the car industry.

Taking our cue from the banking industry, a final point has to be made: concentration *at the European level*, as opposed to the single country level, was anticipated by the executives in the MODEM study rather than observed. Even by the late 1990s, and in spite of the liberalisation of financial services attendant upon the SEM not very much in the way of concentration had occurred. On the other hand there has been a growth in this industry of quasi concentration in the form of intercompany or interbank strategic alliances. Preeminent here are the alliances between the Banco de Santander of Spain and the Royal Bank of Scotland, between the BNP of France and the Dresdener Bank of Germany, as well as alliances between various cooperative and mutual banks in different European countries and cooperation between savings banks. Banking executives also anticipated alliances between banks and insurance companies, some of which have come to pass.

Indeed executives in all the industries were rather voluble on the subject of alliances and loose federations of companies, and there were probably a number of reasons for this, including the developments in banking just indicated and the liberalising effect of the SEM. For some time participants in the car industry have been engaged in intercompany projects and alliances for joint technical development, and more recently coproduction arrangements have been set up. With the benefit of hindsight it may be the case that the managers in question were overimpressed by the strategic alliance between Volvo and Renault. At the time this seemed very remarkable indeed. An alliance between a semispecialist manufacturer of larger cars and one of the bigger generalists, between a government-owned company, Renault, and a private sector company, Volvo; and between two countries popularly thought to be very different in temperament and culture, one of which was a founder member of the Common Market in 1958 the other of which did not join until 1995. But then of course this alliance did not last.

The impact of the SEM

What emerged from the MODEM study was that in predicting and interpreting the implications of the SEM the executives in the study had a different perspective from that of the Eurocrats. Their starting point was different, they emphasised different things and they were less sanguine. While the executives recognised the importance of regulatory harmonisation and the abolition of non-tariff barriers, they were also alive to cultural differences within Europe that would not be affected by the SEM but did have implications for their businesses.

Furthermore they gave pride of place to market forces – factors such as concentration, bipolarisation, segment-specific strategising, competition from non-European countries and so on. The executives tended to see these as more important than anything that could be done by Brussels or individual governments. At the same time they conceded that the SEM would facilitate and encourage existing trends.

The executives were less sanguine than the Eurocrats in that while they expected to make gains as a result of the SEM, they also considered that it would lead to (1) more intense competition (it would be easier for companies/countries to invade each other's markets), which would drive down prices and margins; and (2) end-users would have more choice and become more critical and demanding, which would shorten product life cycles, and raise R&D and promotional costs. Not quite the views expressed in the Cecchini report.

It is probably also helpful to distinguish between the internal and external effects of the SEM, that is, between the impact of the SEM on the strategies and performance of companies within the EU, and its impact on companies in non-

EU countries. With regard to the internal effects, it is very difficult to generalise across industries. The main reason for this is that there is a tension between
the EU on the one hand and European diversity on the other. The European
countries differ from each other in all sorts of ways. But at its inception in 1958
the European Community chose to reduce that difference by intermember
state tariff reduction and a common external tariff, and in 1992 the Single
European Market sought to reduce that difference further by abolishing the
non-tariff barriers mentioned at the start of this discussion. But none of these
measures addressed the question of cultural and institutional diversity in
Europe, and how this diversity impacts differently on the operations, products, services and distribution dynamics of different industries. Furthermore
any attempt at homogenisation will impact differently as well.

One can generalise only to the extent of saying that the SEM has reduced
barriers to free trade within the EU, and will therefore stimulate the development of international strategies and facilitate mergers and acquisitions (although not uniformly in the different countries of the EU). When it comes to
particular industries there are different stories.

Cultural, institutional and indeed language differences are important for
the publishing industry. The SEM has had no impact on these, and has had
little effect on the industry's most culture-dependent segments – fiction and
school books.

In the brewing industry, if the SEM had been followed by price, tax and
VAT harmonisation this would have been a spur to European marketing, but
such harmonisation has not yet occurred. The continuing trend towards European marketing and branding reflects an industry/business dynamic that
both pre- and post- dates the SEM.

In retail banking, the deregulation attendant on the SEM has speeded up
concentration in the industry and facilitated mergers and acquisitions, and
especially alliances.

Clearly the car industry was already Europeanised, or globalised in the case
of some companies: for some years there had been progress on the harmonisation of technical norms, and technical development alliances abound in the
industry. Thus the SEM has not had a major impact on the car industry
although clearly there are some operational and logistical advantages, such as
the greater ease with which components and subassemblies can be moved
around the EU. As a Ford executive interviewed in the study commented:
'1992 began for us in 1967, when we set up Ford of Europe'.

The EU and the wider world

The external effects of the SEM can be depicted in more general terms.
Western Europe is an attractive market to companies in other (non-EU) countries since:

- It is relatively affluent.
- European industry is more fragmented than that of Japan and the USA, which means there are fewer companies in Europe whose market dominance cannot be challenged.
- Western Europe has a large population.
- It can be used as a bridge to Eastern Europe.

Insofar as the SEM has lowered internal barriers, deregulated and promoted regulatory harmonisation, it is encouraging non-EU companies to locate and compete there.

References

Ackermann, K. F. (1988) 'Europe Ahead: the changing role of human resources management in German companies', paper presented at the conference on International Comparisons in Human Resource Management, Cranfield School of Management, UK, September.

Calori, Roland and Peter Lawrence (1991) *The Business of Europe: Managing Change*, London: Sage.

Cecchini, Paolo (1988) *The European Challenge: the Benefits of a Single Market*, Aldershot: Gower.

Dudley, James W. (1989) *1992: Strategies for the Single Market*, Kogan Page: London.

CHAPTER 3

Drink and diversity: the spirit of Europe

There is tension between the standardising intentions of the EU and the cultural heterogeneity of Europe. Rather than simply explore this tension in terms of generalities, we are going to take an industry, one of those referred to in the previous chapter, and look at it in more detail to give some substance to the idea of intercountry difference. The industry is brewing: familiar, long-established and with a user friendly product.

The brewing industry, as suggested in the previous chapter, is marked by some strategic and developmental generalities – segmentation, concentration, bipolarisation and so on – and it will also emerge here that brewing companies increasingly engage in manoeuvres and adaptations that are business driven rather than production driven. Nonetheless brewing does serve very nicely to illuminate *country differences* in Europe. We will consider brewing from the view point of consumption, operations and the relation between brewing and the various national economies.

Consumption

First of all there are quite marked differences in the mix of alcoholic drinks consumed in the various countries, as well as in per capita alcohol consumption. Let us start with volume (Table 3.1).

As well as noting the scale of consumption differences between countries, one might speculate as to why the French drink a lot and the Swedes, relatively speaking, do not: these two countries share joint thirteenth place in Hofstede's famous individualism ratings (Hofstede, 1980).

When one looks at the different kinds of alcohol that make up this crude total, however, rather different orderings emerge (Table 3.2).

TABLE 3.1   Litres of alcohol consumed per head in litres of same alcohol, 1994

France	12.3
Germany	11.9
Austria	11.8
Portugal	11.4
Belgium and Luxembourg	10.6
Denmark	9.9
Spain	9.7
Italy	8.0
Netherlands	7.7
Ireland	7.3
UK	7.0
Finland	6.8
Greece	6.2
Sweden	6.0

Source: Brewers and Licensed Retailers Association, 1995.

TABLE 3.2   Consumption of spirits, wine and beer in descending order, 1994

	Spirits	*Wine*	*Beer*
Highest	Germany	France	Germany
	France	Portugal	Denmark
	Belgium and Luxembourg	Italy	Ireland
	Spain	Spain	Austria
	Finland	Austria	Belgium and Luxembourg
	Netherlands	Denmark	UK
	Austria	Belgium and Luxembourg	Finland
	Sweden	Greece	Netherlands
	Greece	Germany	Spain
	Ireland	Netherlands	Portugal
	UK	UK	Sweden
	Denmark	Sweden	Greece
	Portugal	Finland	France
Lowest	Italy	Ireland	Italy

Source: Brewers and Licensed Retailers Association, 1995.[a]

Interestingly, no one country comes high on all three lists, or low on all of them; using this ordinal measure the Swedes again appear to be the most restrained.

If we enquire into whether the beer drinkers drink draft, or bottled or canned beer, using a different source and a more limited range of EU countries, then a different ordering emerges (Table 3.3). The mighty Germans, whose per capita beer consumption towers within in the EU, are defeated 4 to 1 by the Irish when it comes to drinking draft beer.

The draft versus non-draft propensity in turn has implications for where beer is bought and where it is consumed. Draft beer is consumed in hotels, restaurants, cafés, clubs, and above all in bars and public houses. The table above reflects the café style trends among draft enthusiasts, the predominance of the pub in Britain and in Ireland, and of the bar-café in Spain and Portugal. In contrast most non-draft beer is bought in shops, clubs, supermarkets and, in Britain, off-licenses, and is consumed at home. Among the serious beer drinkers, at least among the British, Germans and Irish, one can see a gentle trend away from draft beer (Table 3.4).

Among the traditional beer-drinking countries, in Belgium and the Netherlands consumption was stable over this period, although in Denmark there was a modest increase in the proportion of draft beer consumed, albeit from a very low base. Particularly striking is the 10 per cent reduction in the relative proportion of draft beer consumed in the UK, the land of the public house. This change is often ascribed to the growing concern with safe driving, leading to more drinking at home. There may, however, be other factors at work here.

British brewers have traditionally brewed top-fermented, darker coloured beers – ales (bitter) and stout – rather than the lighter coloured, bottom-

TABLE 3.3 Percentage of draft beer consumed, 1995

Ireland	82
UK	67
Belgium	40
Spain	37
Portugal	32
Holland	31
France	24
Germany	22
Italy	16
Denmark	7
Greece	4

Source: Confédération des Brasseurs du Marché Commun (CBMC), 1995.

TABLE 3.4   Percentage of draft beer consumed, 1985–94

	1985	1987	1988	1989	1992	1994
Ireland	88	88	86	86	83	82
UK	77	75	73	72	70	67
Germany	29	29	28	28	22	22

Source: Conféderation des Brasseurs du Marché Commun (CBMC), 1995.

fermented lagers favoured on the continent. But British taste has moved from ale/bitter and stout to a majority preference for lager. By 1995, 45.2 per cent of beer consumed in the UK was ales and stout and the remaining 54.8 per cent was lager. While ale and stout still constitute a slightly higher proportion of *draft* beer consumption, when it comes to *packaged* beer (cans or bottles) over 70 per cent is lager. The switch in taste from darker beers to lager in turn raises the question of how this changing demand has been met. There are three answers:

- By British brewers brewing continental or other lagers under license.
- By a (belated) production of a few British lager brands.
- By importing foreign lagers.

British retailers, especially supermarket chains, responded energetically to the challenge of satisfying the growing preference for lager by offering a very wide selection of canned and bottled lagers of all three kinds, together with own-label lagers sourced both at home and abroad. It seems likely that this very wide supermarket offering of lager has contributed to the move away from draft beer drinking in pubs to lager drinking at home.

Returning to the wider theme of the differences between the European and especially the EU countries, it is not only the draft versus canned/bottled ratio that differs, but also the nature of the bottles. Beer is sold in both returnable and non-returnable bottles, and the proportions sold in cans, returnable bottles and non-returnable bottles are very different between countries (Table 3.5).

First Denmark and then Germany adopted a returnable bottles system, on environmental grounds, and the Netherlands is close to the same end. All the other countries, however, allow the use of non-returnable bottles, that is, bottles that are discarded when the beer has been drunk; and Britain, as always the most Americanised of the European countries, followed by Ireland, offers the bulk if its packaged beer in metal cans.

When it comes to trends in consumption then, CBMC data over the period 1980–95 shows a lack of consistency, with countries peaking, declining and

TABLE 3.5   Domestic beer sales by contraction, 1994

	Returnable bottles	Non-returnable bottles	Cans
Germany	100	–	–
Denmark	100	–	–
Belgium	88	7	5
UK	12	18	70
Ireland	22	22	56
Holland	93	7	–
Spain	59	30	11
Portugal	81	13	6
Greece	79	4	17
France	21	72	7
Italy	18	69	13

Source: Adapted from CBMC, 1995.

sometimes rising again. France for example had its highest per capita beer consumption in 1990, then consumption declined before peaking again in 1996, followed by another decline. Ireland peaked in 1992 and then declined; the Netherlands peaked in 1991 and thereafter declined.

However one trend is just about perceptible. Some but not all of the traditional beer-drinking countries – Belgium and Luxembourg, Denmark, Germany and Britain showed a slight decline over the 1980–95 period, while at the same time two non-traditional beer-drinking countries – Italy and Portugal – showed a slight increase. Beer drinking tends to have a different meaning in these warmer southern European countries – it is seen more as a means of quenching one's thirst and is thus in competition with soft drinks rather than wine or spirits. Again it is possible that beer drinking in southern Europe will be boosted by health concerns and the antialcohol lobby since it has both 'a better image' and a lower alcohol to volume ratio.

What has emerged in this first section is a picture of considerable variety among the EU countries, or subsets of them, in just about every measurable aspect of beer consumption. A similar picture emerges when it comes to production.

Production

The parameters of production are variable when one compares the various European (mostly EU) countries. Starting with the number of breweries per country, this is not only variable but randomly variable (Table 3.6).

TABLE 3.6   **Structure of brewing industry, 1994**

	No. of independent brewing companies	*No. of breweries (plants)*
Belgium	91	106
Denmark	9	15
Germany	1200	1243
Spain	13	24
France	22	26
Greece	3	5
Ireland	3	7
Italy	6	18
Luxembourg	5	5
Netherlands	15	17
Austria	48	54
Portugal	4	8
Finland	5	8
Sweden	23	26
UK	64	93

Source: CBMC, 1995.

TABLE 3.7   **Level of concentration**

	Industry situation	*Number of competitors*	*Share of market (%)*
Denmark	Monopoly	1	71
Netherlands	Monopoly	1	74
Italy	Monopoly	2	61
Belgium	Monopoly	2	86
France	Monopoly	2	71
UK	Concentrated	5	84
Spain	Concentrated	5	87
Germany	Fragmented	5	26

Source: Jacobs and Steele, 1997.

Table 3.6 reveals a dynamic anomaly – while Germany does have the largest population, highest consumption and biggest output, the number of breweries is still out of all proportion (see later data on concentration). Furthermore the country with the second largest number of brewing companies/plants is not the second largest country (Britain) but 'gallant little Belgium'.

Looking at a more restricted range of EU countries (Table 3.7), it emerges that there are some significant differences in the level of concentration (see Chapter 1).

Intriguingly there is no obvious connection between concentration and country size, consumption level or even productivity – the two countries with the highest degree of concentration – Denmark and the Netherlands – have a middle of the range output per employee. Similarly the production figures for the various EU countries are varied and do not correlate with population, apart from the fact that Germany is in the lead (Table 3.8).

Readers should note that although Germany and Britain have the largest output, taste and export capability explain some of the variation between countries: while Britain and Italy have similar population sizes the British output exceeds that of Italy five to one! It all becomes clearer when one identifies the top brewing companies (Table 3.9). The distribution of the top brands is loosely consistent with the listing of top brewers (Table 3.10).

Heineken has two of the top five brands (Heineken and Amstel) and Carlsberg has two of the top ten (Carlsberg and Tuborg – these brewing companies merged in 1970). Kronenbourg is the principal brand of the French food and drinks conglomerate Danone. When it comes to cross-border owner-ship there is a clear association between the size and scale of the brewing company and the likelihood that it will own, wholly or partly, a brewing plant in another European country. The top four brewing companies in terms of cross-border ownership are Heineken, Danone, Carlsberg and Interbrew (Table 3.11). They are also among the top six in terms of output, as shown in Table 3.9. Heineken, Europe's largest brewing company, is the most active in cross-border ownership.

TABLE 3.8   Beer production by country, 1994

	1995 production in 1000 hectolitres
Belgium	14488
Denmark	10058
Germany	117400
Spain	25313
France	20634
Greece	4009
Ireland	7402
Italy	11990
Luxembourg	518
Netherlands	23118
Austria	9662
Portugal	6928
Finland	4756
Sweden	5309
UK	56800

Source: CBMC, 1995.

TABLE 3.9   Estimated sales of top brewers, 1994

Brewer	Sales in millions of hectolitres
Heineken (Netherlands)	60.4
Carlsberg (Denmark)	30.2
Danone (France)	26.7
Guinness (Eire)	25.6
Bass (UK)	16.4
Interbrew (Belgium)	14.7
Courage (UK)*	12.2
Oetker (Germany)	9.6
Brau & Brunnen (Germany)	9.4
Maerz (Germany)	9.3
Whitbread (UK)	7.8
Holsten (Germany)	7.8
Scottish & Newcastle (UK)*	6.9
Grolsch (Netherlands)	2.1

*In 1995 Courage and Scottish & Newcastle merged to become Scottish Courage.
Source: Jacobs and Steele, 1997, in turn based on annual reports and trade sources.

TABLE 3.10   Top 10 European brands in the early 1990s

1. Heineken	6. Aquila Pils
2. Carlsberg	7. Skol
3. Kronenbourg	8. Stella Artois
4. Guinness	9. San Miguel
5. Amstel	10. Tuborg

Source: Jacobs and Steel, 1997.

Another point of interest is that Germany, by far the biggest market (see Table 3.2), has attracted little investment from foreign brewers. German beer drinkers are wildly patriotic, and there are a staggering array of German brands and brewers to cater to their needs. Not only are there over 1200 breweries in Germany (see Table 3.6), indeed there are 800 breweries in Bavaria alone, but 90 per cent of German breweries sell their products within a 30 mile radius. This state of affairs is in part the result of the famous *Reinheitsgebot* (purity laws, introduced in 1516, although they did not become standard for the whole of Germany until the time of the First World War). These purity laws state that all beer must be made from just four pure ingredients: malted cereals, yeast, water and of course hops. There can be no

TABLE 3.11   Cross-border ownership, leading European breweries

	Heineken	*Danone*	*Carlsberg*	*Interbrew*
France	*	**		*
Germany			*	
Belgium		*		**
Holland	**			
Denmark			**	
Spain	*	*	*	
Italy	*	*	*	
Greece	*	*		
UK			*	
Ireland	*			

* Ownership presence.
** Country of origin.

TABLE 3.12   Productivity per employee in brewing industry in different countries

	Output per employee 1000 hectolitres
Portugal	3.65
Italy	3.48
Ireland	3.43
France	3.28
Netherlands	2.78
Spain	2.58
Denmark	2.42
Germany	2.39
Greece	2.10
Belgium	2.07
UK	1.93
Finland	1.79
Luxembourg	1.69
Austria	1.61
Sweden	1.42

artificial additives to enhance flavour, nor to extend shelf life, which inhibits the transportation of beer over long distances. With regard to imported beer, in 1987 the European Court of Justice ruled that the *Reinheitsgebot* could not be invoked to prevent the sale of imported beers in Germany, but this ruling has made little difference in practice since imported (and therefore 'unpure') beers have to be clearly labelled as such, and traditional German beer drinkers are very loyal to their native brewers and local brands. One of the few non-

European brewers to enter Germany is Fosters, although the product is marked 'brewed in Hamburg in accordance with the Germany purity laws'.

As Table 3.11 makes clear, much the same is true of Denmark, although this attracts less attention since Denmark has a much smaller and, to foreign exporters, less attractive national market. Furthermore male Danish drinkers are pretty conservative and do not favour foreign beers: whenever Danish brewers have sought to introduce a foreign beer under licence, Budwieser for example, it has been a flop – and one has the feeling that everyone was jolly pleased.

Finally, with regard to beer production the productivity figures for the different EU countries also show considerable variation (Table 3.12). It would seem that the Mediterranean countries are better at making beer than drinking it!

Brewing and the contribution to the national economy

The brewing industry clearly impacts on the various national economies in a number of small ways: it provides employment, contributes to government revenue via taxes and duties, contributes to the nation's trade balance and in some cases provokes cross-border shopping on a significant scale – even smuggling.

Unlike car production and retail banking, brewing is not a major generator of employment. Nonetheless it provides significant employment in two of the EU countries, according to CBMC statistics for 1995. The two countries are Germany, where some 49000 people work in brewing, and the UK, with 29000. And given their relatively small populations it is worth adding that some 4190 people work in brewing in Denmark, some 7000 in Belgium and some 8310 in Holland.

While the Germans lead in beer consumption, their export record is relatively modest. It is the Netherlands – with the mighty Heineken, supported by the redoubtable Grolsch – that heads the list (Table 3.13). Note the enormous gap between the four leaders and the rest of the EU countries.

Clearly the impact of brewing as an export earner varies massively across the EU countries. Those that score well are small countries that are lucky enough to have one or more large and successful brewers within their borders, so that the contribution of Carlsberg, Interbrew, Guiness and above all Heineken is paramount. In another set of countries beer production is primarily to satisfy the national demand, a demand that is usually fairly modest though growing in some cases – this group includes Spain, Portugal, Italy, France, Finland and Sweden.

We said above that two countries are clearly anomalous: Britain and Germany. Britain is undoubtedly a traditional beer-drinking country – its

TABLE   3.13   Proportion   of   national   beer
production that is exported, 1994

	Per cent
Netherlands	44.8
Ireland	44.0
Belgium and Luxembourg	31.3
Denmark	30.6
Portugal	10.4
France	6.9
Germany	6.5
Finland	6.4
Greece	5.7
UK	5.2
Italy	3.7
Spain	1.4

Note: No figures are available for Sweden and Austria.
Source: CBMC, 1995.

pubs are world famous and a major tourist attraction. Its beer consumption is high, albeit slowly declining, and its total production is second only to that of Germany. Yet a mere 5 per cent of this production is exported. The reason for this, as stated in the section on consumption, is the traditional British taste for top-fermented, darker ales or bitter, while the rest of the world prefers bottom-fermented, lighter coloured lager beers. Nowadays more lager is being drunk in Britain than bitter, but the greater proportion of lager is imported or brewed under licence. British brewers have developed some native lager brands, but they have served as import substitutes rather than exports, so that it tends to be only speciality beers of the Newcastle Brown kind that find their way into other countries.

The case of Germany is even more intriguing. It produces more beer than any other country in the world except the USA, drinks more per head that any of its EU partners, has more brewers and more brands that anyone else, but exports only a paltry 6.5 per cent of production. As we have seen, the famous *Reinhietsgebot* or purity laws serve to keep foreign beer out, but do they in some way keep German beer in? Or is it rather that brewing in Germany has had the aura and *modus operandi* of a cottage industry until the last decade of the twentieth century? As discussed above, the brewing industry in Germany is rather fragmented, and what little concentration has occurred has been a feature of the 1990s. Calori and Lawrence (1991) have also noted that lower levels of profitability exist for many German brewers – lower than would be acceptable in Britain.

The corresponding issue – the extent to which imported beer figures in the consumption of the various EU countries – shows less in the way of interesting variation. The EU average is 6.3 per cent. The country that consumes the least imported beer is, as one might expect, Denmark at 1.8 per cent (CBMC, 1995). It is a small country, dominated by a world-class brewery but with several secondary breweries. The Danes are also well known, like the Germans, as 'patriotic drinkers'. The two countries with the highest proportion of imported beer are France at 16.9 per cent and Italy at 17.5 per cent. Both these countries, and particularly Italy, are probably affected by cross-border ownership, in part illuminated in Table 3.11. Britain records a figure of 8.7 per cent for imported beer, though this in a sense underestimates Britain's dependence on the beer of other countries since much of the lager consumed in Britain is brewed under licence. For example the leading British brewer, Whitbread, brews both Heineken and Stella Artois under licence.

If one turns to the question of who buys whose beer – that is, which countries import from which other countries – a fascinating patchwork emerges. If we restrict ourselves to the countries that export reasonable amounts, the picture comes out as shown in Table 3.14.

One theme running through Table 3.14 is what one might call 'twins and neighbours'. Britain and Ireland are beer-trading twins; Denmark exports most to the only country with which it has a common border – Germany; Belgium exports most to the three countries with which it has borders – Holland, France and Germany; and 'island fortress Britain' sends more beer to its twin countries just across the sea – France and Ireland – than to anywhere else. A secondary theme here is that Italy and France are too weak to resist!

When it comes to export sales outside Europe, Asia and the USA are the two most attractive markets. Apart from Ireland, all the leading exporters shown on Table 3.13 have significant sales in Asia, all of them sell some beer to the USA, and three of the countries have sizeable sales in the USA: Netherlands (3806 thousand hectolitres), Germany (1132 thousand hectolitres) and Britain

TABLE 3.14   **Cross-country exports in beer**

	Exporting countries					
	Belgium and Luxembourg	*Denmark*	*Germany*	*Ireland*	*Holland*	*UK*
Top three importing countries and amounts in 1000 hectolitres	France: 2077 Netherlands: 1104 Germany: 464	Germany: 1267 Italy: 412 Belgium and Luxembourg: 123	Italy: 1154 UK: 1423 France: 620	UK: 2790 Germany: 94 France: 36	Spain: 1159 UK: 664 Germany: 409	Ireland: 419 France: 301 Italy: 267

Source: CBMC, 1995.

(871 thousand hectolitres) (CBMC, 1995). The most startling fact to emerge from this comparison is that Dutch sales to the USA exceed German sales by about three to one. Heineken, the brewer that is largely responsible for this national achievement, certainly enjoyed 'first mover advantage' with regard to the American market. On 14 April 1933 the *New York Times* reported the first legal shipment of beer in thirteen years (the Prohibition period): 100 gallons was shipped from the Heineken brewery in Rotterdam to Hoboken, New Jersey – and this was less than six weeks after Roosevelt's famous 'nothing to fear but fear' inauguration speech. In 1994 the USA took 37 per cent of the Netherlands' total beer production.

The import–export patchwork shown in Table 3.13 is no doubt in part a reflection of cross-border ownership. Here there is a pattern. The traditional beer-producing countries – Denmark, Holland, Belgium, Germany and Britain – have largely escaped foreign implantations and acquisitions, while the leading non-traditional beer producers – Spain and Italy – have experienced a good deal of foreign participation in their brewing. France is in an in – between position. The top five brewers in Spain are in part foreign owned (Table 3.15).

A similar pattern is discernible in Italy (Table 3.16).

According to Jacobs and Steele (1997) France is between the two extremes – the largest brewer is Danone (Kronenbourg), the second largest is a Heineken subsidiary, the third largest an Interbrew subsidiary, and the next two, Brasserie Fischer and Brasserie St Omer, are French.

Finally in this consideration of the impact of brewing on national economies is the question of how much taxation revenue is generated by the industry. Such revenue is substantial in the case of Germany (modest taxation but high consumption) and enormous in the case of the UK (high consumption and high taxation). Indeed the **variations** in VAT and excise duty on beer around the EU are marked, and have been more strikingly anomalous since the implementation of the Single European Market.

TABLE 3.15   **Ownership of the top five Spanish brewers**

Brewer	*Ownership*
Cruzcampo	89% Guinness, 11% Carlsberg
El Aguila	65% Heineken
Mahon	33% Danone of France
Danim	16% Oetker of Germany, 5% San Miguel
San Miguel	Affiliated to San Miguel in the Philippines, 25% owned by Danone

Source: Jacobs and Steele, 1997.

TABLE 3.16   Ownership of the top four Italian brewers

Brewer	Ownership
Peroni	25% Danone
Dreher-Heineken	100% Heineken
Poretti	50% Carlsberg
Moretti	Created when it and another brewer, Prinz, were bought and merged by Labatts of Canada, now itself acquired by Interbrew of Belgium

Source: Jacobs and Steele, 1997.

In two cases the taxation differences between countries have given rise to significant cross-border trade based on private initiative. The first case is that of Denmark and Germany. Danes regularly cross into Germany to buy cheap beer (and petrol), but the beer they buy is Danish beer, thoughtfully supplied to German retailers by Danish brewers, thus escaping the high taxation on beer in Denmark. Although the taxes are high in Denmark, they are higher in Sweden and higher still in Finland.

The British do not compare themselves with the Danes, Swedes or Finns in terms of VAT and excise duty, but with the French, and the tax difference between the two countries has led since 1992 to a cross-border *cause célèbre*. According to the BLRA's *Tax Facts* pamphlet (BLRA, 1995b), the total tax on beer in Britain is more that seven times higher than in France: 30p a pint in Britain compared with 4p a pint in France. The BLRA claims that the beer trade from France to Britain is running at around 1.1 million pints a day, about a third of which comes across in hired vans and much of which is sold illegally at car boot sales, on housing estates and even door to door. This phenomenon is of course only a small part of the European brewing scene, but it is an idiosyncratic and odd postscript to the Single Market.

The Anglo-French beer duty scam also serves to remind us that while in European matters all the countries are different, Britain is 'more different than the others'. Consider the following:

- Only Britain (and Ireland) are traditional dark-beer-drinking countries.
- The switch in preference to lager beers by the British public left British brewers largely unable to export and vulnerable to quasi-imports (alone among the traditional beer-drinking countries).
- Britain sells a large proportion of its beer in cans (see Table 3.5), much larger than any of the other EU countries.

- Britain's draft beer consumption is second only to that of Ireland (see Table 3.3).
- Britain and Ireland have a close beer-trading relationship, and no other country is close to Ireland in terms of trade or consumption.
- Britain has a substantial link between production and distribution in the sense of 'tied houses' (pubs owned by breweries and mandated to sell only those beers ordained by the brewer), although the extent of the tie has been reduced on the recommendation of the Monopolies and Mergers Commission; only Germany has a similar tied system.
- The British brewing industry is not very concentrated compared with Denmark, Holland, Italy, Belgium and France; this is remarkable in a business-conscious national community emphasising shareholder value.

On top of all this Britain's pubs are a national institution. In a BLRA survey (BLRA, 1995b), nine out of ten foreign visitors to the UK said they wanted to visit a pub, and 85 per cent of those who expressed an opinion said that British pubs were better than the bars in their own country. Among the British themselves, eight out of ten adults count themselves as pub-goers, and 29 per cent visit a pub at least once a week. Again in a BLRA survey (BLRA, 1995b), 27 per cent of those questioned had either met their partners or had their first date in a pub.

This too reflects the inability of the EU to address cultural difference.

References

Brewers and Licensed Retailers Association (BLRA) (1995a) *Statistical Handbook*, London: Brewing Publications Limited.

Brewers and Licensed Retailers Association (BLRA) (1995b) *Beer and Pub Facts*, London: Brewing Publications Limited.

Brewing and Licensed Retailers Association (BLRA) (1995c) *Tax Facts*, London: Brewing Publications Limited.

Calori, Roland and Peter Lawrence (1991) *The Business of Europe*, London: Sage.

Confédération des Brasseurs du Marché Commun (CBMC) (1995) *Statistiques*, Brussels: CBMC.

Hofstede, G (1980) *Cultures Consequences*, Beverly Hills, Los Angeles: Sage.

Jacobs, Tony and Murray Steele (1997) 'The European Brewing Industry', unpublished case study, Cranfield School of Management.

CHAPTER 4

Patterns and forces

In probing the nature of EU-dominated Europe we have so far identified three forces. Two of these are forces for standardisation, or at least for cross-border operation. The third force is the persistence of national differences.

The first force is of course the EU itself. From its inception as the EEC in 1958 it imposed policy and regulatory uniformity on different national units. The Single European Market initiative, discussed in Chapter 1, has taken this process further by eliminating non-tariff barriers, or at least having a jolly good try, and facilitating cross-border procurement, manufacture and distribution.

The second force is rather more subtle in its origin and effect. It is the recognition by senior executives that the operations of their companies are at least regional (where a region equals a group of countries) if not international or global. As a consequence they frame cross-border strategies for their companies, and they take cognizance of a variety of business developments of a European or international nature, such as trends towards segmentation, bipolarisation, concentration, Europeanisation and so on. All this surfaced in Chapter 2 when we tried both to put the Single European Market initiative into contest and to depart from an exclusively 'Eurocratic' view of it by citing a survey of a hundred or so executives from seven EU countries (that is, seven out of the twelve member countries at the time the research was conducted in the early 1990s). The essence of the executives' view is that business is a global game marked by global trends. Business will take cognizance of national frontiers when it has to, but national differences are seen as constraints.

In Chapter 3 we took the opposite perspective by starting with an ensemble of EU countries and asking whether they are the same or whether there are interesting differences. To make this comparison both meaningful and specific we concentrated on a single industry, brewing, one of the industries whose executives contributed to the strategic generalities presented in the previous chapter. As we have seen, when one considers the individual countries, and not the views of strategically generalising executives, all sorts of differences emerge. In this instance differences in taste, and consumption emerged, as did differences in the contribution made by the brewing industry to the various national economies in terms of employment, tax revenue and the balance of trade.

So the third force is the persistence of national differences despite the best efforts of Brussels Eurocrats and globally strategising executives. These differences are cultural, institutional and regulatory. They are also shot through with happenstance in the sense that the EU countries have histories as separate states and therefore bring different things to the feast of European union. None of this is to contradict the viewpoint of the executives. Concentration and bipolarisation do indeed characterise the brewing industry, but at the end of the day Guinness is Irish, Heineken is Dutch and the French prefer wine anyway!

In the present chapter we shall adjust the angle of vision again and focus not on countries or executives, but on industries, that are represented in a variety of EU countries. We shall look at four industries (chocolate and confectionery, footwear, insulated cables, and paint) that figured in a multicountry, EU-funded study directed by ESC Lyon (France) in the mid 1990s. This chapter is complementary to the previous one. It takes each industry as the *point de départ* and asks, whether patterns, similarities and common elements exist, or whether the whole affair is a patchwork of national differences.

Cables

We shall start with cables because it is the only one of the four industries that has a range of wholly industrial products, hence there can be no question of nationally biased differences in consumer taste and any cross-border patterns should show up.

The ESC study covered companies in the four named industries in Britain, France, Germany, Italy, the Netherlands, Spain and Sweden, and also in the USA to provide a non-European comparison, and proceeded in terms of a senior executive interview and a questionnaire survey. All the executives interviewed were asked how their industries were segmented. The cable industry executives from the various countries tended to segment the industry in broadly similar ways, where again a segment is a subset of products and/or customers that may have different dynamics or behavioural patterns. The executives tended to divide the industry into segments according to technology and application, *viz.*:

- Energy and power cables.
- Telecommunications.

- Automobile (car wiring).
- Measuring/controlling cables.
- Domestic installation.
- Speciality products/special applications.

There was also loose agreement on the nature of competition within these segments. Cables used for domestic installation constitute a local or national market. Power cables, on the other hand, are a national market in the process of being transformed into a regional one, where a region represents a group of countries. In Europe the market for telecommunication cables has traditionally been national, with national PTTs as the principal purchasers, but this is also becoming cross-border, largely in the wake of the single European market requirement for EU-wide competitive tendering for public procurement together with the deregulation of telecommunication service provision. The markets for the various speciality cables are variable in their competitive structure, for instance the market for measuring and controlling cables is international, and so on. There was also a general agreement among the executives questioned that purchasing structure determines the nature of competition. In simple terms the question is, who is the customer? Is it a particular country's national government, some other country's government, a company, or some other entity? And again there was a common perception among the executives that the greater the value-added of the product, the more likely it is that the competition will be global.

There was also agreement on developments in the industry and the directions the industry is expected to take, including:

- The concentration of companies in order to promote economies of scale (a now familiar theme) and promote access to markets in other countries.
- A search for new markets, driven by the decline or saturation of European markets.
- The emergence of markets in developing countries.
- The partial deregulation of telecommunications is causing a proliferation of buyers (in place of a *single* public authority for each country).

There was also recognition that in several segments the emphasis may shift from supplying cables to supplying systems that *include* cables, along the lines of 'the intelligent building'. This in turn may well lead to a shift from production-based value-added to design-based value-added.

So far so good. There was broad agreement among the representatives of the cable industry with regard to industry segmentation, the nature of the segments, and the key issues and developments. At the same time it has to be admitted that an industry where the buyers are mostly other companies is likely to favour the identification of an industry pattern rather than a national patchwork. But what of chocolate?

Chocolate and confectionery

Firstly, it is desirable to separate chocolate from confectionery as they are different industries in several ways, even if some companies produce both. Confectionery is much more traditional, much less international, and something of a British speciality. In particular Britain is the home of the boiled sweet. Britain has more companies making boiled sweets than any other country, and they produce primarily for domestic consumption. There has been relatively little invasion of the British sweet market by foreign producers, although British boiled sweets are sold abroad as a rather quaint British speciality. In contrast the chocolate industry is more international, more concentrated and more competitive. In the survey there was broad cross-country agreement on the nature of segmentation, namely:

- Countlines (for example Kit-Kat, Mars, Snickers, Marathon, and so on).
- bars or slabs of chocolate.
- Boxed chocolates of various kinds.
- Some country-based specialities, for example Italy has more seasonal chocolate products, Spain has chocolate with almonds.

Most of the interviewed executives identified the same range of industry developments, including concentration first at national level and then at regional level, paralleled by the Europeanisation of distribution and Europe-wide purchasing. A drive to generate new products was seen as a feature of the recent past. In addition the industry had made an effort to produce global brands, especially in countlines, heavily supported by promotional activity.

Looking to the future, the executives anticipated a continuation of the trend towards industry concentration, and continuing concentration of retail distribution in the sense of more retail chains and fewer independent, old-fashioned sweet shops. It was also anticipated that products would have a shorter shelf life, and that health concerns would increasingly impact upon the industry and might also spur the development of more specialised products, particularly sugar-free and low-fat products. Health concerns seemed to be more prominent in the northern European countries than in the Mediterranean countries, but this might change before the end of the century. Greater specialisation of production was also expected, in terms of one factory making a single product for a whole region.

There was also a general conviction that prices would be increasingly forced down, partly because of competition and partly because of a shift in 'the balance of power' from manufacture to retail, accompanied by retailers' own-label products being sold at a lower price than the manufacturers' branded versions. Another twist to the erosion of margins argument was the recognition that chain retailers were increasingly entering the top end of the market (high-price, quality products) where traditionally they had been the price-competitive sellers of uniformly packaged boiled sweets. A nice example of the last two trends combined – top-end entry and own label – is offered by Britain's Marks & Spencer, who sell chocolates made by Godiva under the St Michael label.

The interviewees thought there was not much scope for market development in Western Europe. As one executive put it: 'I don't see how anyone could get the Belgians to eat more chocolate.' On the other hand market growth opportunities were recognised in Eastern Europe and South America. In the mid 1990s confectionery was a £45 billion market, and consumption in the top 10 countries accounted for over 70 per cent of the total. The countries that made up this top ten are not necessarily the ones you would expect, that is, rich countries where there is a tradition of eating chocolate, such as Austria, Switzerland and Belgium. From a marketing viewpoint these countries have the fatal weakness of being small. Rather the top 10 list includes countries such as Brazil, Russia and the Ukraine.

Returning for a moment to the theme of concentration, an unusual feature of the chocolate industry, irrespective of the country in which the leading companies are headquartered, is that there exists the possibility of further concentration *at the very top*. The top six are Nestlé, Mars, Philip Morris, Cadbury, Ferrero Rocher and Hershey, three of which are American and three Western European. This list is unusual in that only three are quoted companies in the usual sense of large corporations with traded shares: Hershey is a trust and therefore cannot be bought or sold, and Mars and Ferrero Rocher are private, family-owned companies. With a family company there is always the possibility that one or more family members will want or need to sell their shares as a result of a family disagreement, a costly divorce or whatever.

Again the possibility of merger or acquisition 'at the top' is perhaps encouraged by the different degrees of internationalisation among the big players, combined with the difficulty of making headway in a mature market other than by acquisition. So Mars and Nestlé are very international; Philip Morris is mainly active in Europe (at least with regard to its chocolate and confectionery interests); Ferrero Rocher is Italian but its market is primarily in Germany and Italy; Cadbury is traditionally strong in British and Commonwealth markets; while 82 per cent of Hershey's sales are in the USA. All this points to an incentive for concentration.

In summary, while confectionery may seem a less propitious industry than insulated cables for the identification of cross-border similarities, there does seem to be a core of common issues, concerns, expectations and understanding of segmentation.

Footwear

In the footwear industry the situation is more complicated in the sense that more distinctions are made with regard to sources of supply, location of manufacture, differences of taste and differentiation of markets. At the same time, when executives from companies in different countries were interviewed they tended to make the same distinctions, again underlining the tendency for industry-specific consensus to emerge.

Footwear is an industry marked by distinctions. The leading manufacturers are European or American, but raw materials come from a variety of sources. Portugal, Morocco, Greece, Turkey and Tunisia supply the bottom and middle sections of the market. France, Italy and Spain are important markets for everything, and suppliers at the luxury end of the industry. The rest of continental Europe is mainly a market, though Britain is both an important market and a significant producer. Outside Europe, China, Malaysia, Indonesia and India are suppliers and important markets. The rest of Asia largely supplies bottom-end products and sports shoes.

Offshore manufacturing is an industry-wide development, and this even applies to speciality and top-end products. Start-rite in Britain, a quality, specialist manufacturer of children's shoes, has some of its manufacturing carried out in Thailand; or to give a non-European example, Johnson & Murphy in the USA, a very upmarket manufacturer, has some of the work done in Mexico. Offshore manufacture in general poses a quality control challenge to the Euro-American companies that are engaged in it; a challenge to which they have variously responded with rigorous specifications, close inspections, sanctions and in some cases on-site expatriate quality engineers.

The nature of competition varies between industry segments, so that competition is global at the top end (high-quality products such as Gucci), and for branded sportswear products. For other segments competition tends to be national.

There are differences in taste and style within Europe, but they tend to be latitudinal rather than country to country. For example southern European women tend to be shorter and are likely to want shoes with higher heels. Indeed gender differences abound in the footwear industry and can be more important than differences of nationality. For example men buy with a view to the future, women for the short term; that is, men regard shoes as an investment but women are more likely to see them as a fashion item. Men are not especially price sensitive when buying shoes, but women tend to be the opposite. However both men and women are very price sensitive when it comes to buying shoes for their children.

The shift in 'the balance of power' between manufacturer and retailer is not as marked as in the chocolate and confectionery industry, but it is perceptible and is most marked in Britain. The emerging pattern is as follows:

- The progressive elimination of independent retailers stocking the products of various manufacturers.
- The growth of retail chains, forcing manufacturers' margins down and competition up, sometimes exerting pressure for own-label products.
- Some major manufacturers are responding by establishing their own retail outlets.

This last development, vertical integration forward, albeit only partial, was also recognised in some cases in the chocolate industry. Here Godiva provides a good example as it not only has its own retail outlets, but these are positioned in very prestigious locations, for instance in the Rue St Honoré in Paris, in Regent Street in London and in the Beverley Hills Mall in Los Angeles.

So with regard to footwear, while there are a range of distinctions to be made these tend to be distinctions within the industry rather than country-specific formulations, again supporting the idea of a loose consensus on industry issues and developments.

Paint and varnish

The last industry we want to review from the standpoint of trying to identify clusters of industry concerns and perceptions that are not tied to particular countries of operation or location – paint – is both a consumer goods industry and an industrial goods industry. That is to say, all the interviewed executives distinguished sharply between decorative paints for building interiors and exteriors, and industrial paint, irrespective of whether their companies made both. It is perhaps not accurate to describe decorative paints as 'consumer goods' since there are a number of buyers:

- Members of the general public who wish to paint their own homes.
- Self-employed painters who decorate private houses.
- Other bodies with a responsibility to paint buildings, for example school authorities.

Again among the interviewed executives there was consensus that the industrial side is made up of a number of discrete segments, including paints for vehicles, aeroplanes, ships, containers and so on. There was also agreement that competition tends to be global in these industrial segments, and that this is driven by the needs of large corporate customers, for example breweries and soft drinks producers. It was also recognised that markets for speciality paints are global too.

While the above account depicts the industry structure in general terms, there are some departures. Not all users of industrial paint are global Coca Cola type companies with a uniform and uniformly packaged product. The furniture industry, for instance, is highly fragmented, and there has been some fragmentation of buying power in some countries as a result of budgetary devolution: in Britain, for example, the Ministry of Defence is no longer the sole buyer in the defence sector.

With regard to decorative paints, there was general agreement that there are regional differences of taste and need within Europe, but as with footwear these tend to be latitudinal rather than country by country. The demand for stains, varnishes and non-gloss paints for the treatment of wood is greater in Northern Europe than in the South. But Southern Europe has a differentiated demand for:

- Masonry paint (for stone walls and buildings).
- Mosquito repellent paint.
- Thermal paint that will cool in summer and warm in winter.

The interviewees recognised that environmental pressure and legislation will have an increasing impact on the industry. Environmental pressure in particular will cause a move away from solvent-based paints to water-based paints and powdered paints. Environmental pressure is more marked in Northern Europe than in the South, and, this is causing a short-term market incongruence. As one Swedish executive put it: 'Varnish made in Spain could not be sold in Sweden.' Furthermore environmental pressure is leading to some relocation of production to areas with less stringent environmental controls, for example from Australia to Asia.

The environmental issue is also tending to divide the decorative from the industrial segments, in the sense that there is a tension between quality, effectiveness and cost on the one hand and environmental acceptability on the other. Industrial users tend to be more critical of the effectiveness of water-based paints and argue that they are less time and cost effective in that more than one coat may be needed.

When it comes to manufacturing under licence there is some country patterning along 'zones of influence' lines, typically reflecting countries' colonial ties or international alignments, so that:

- Latin America manufactures under licence from the USA.
- Former colonies in British Africa manufacture under licence from Britain.
- Former colonies in French Africa manufacture under licence from France.
- Asia manufactures under licence from Japan.
- Eastern Europe manufactures under licence from Germany.

As always concentration is a recognised development in the industry, with petroleum and chemical companies moving into paint, for example Total of France and Akzo-Nobel of the Netherlands, and as with the other industries reviewed a growth in retailer power was noted by the interviewees with regard to the decorative paint segment. There is, however, a further twist that tends to reinforce the north versus south difference: DIY (do it yourself) stores have long been restricted to the Northern European countries, although they are now spreading to Southern Europe. It is in DIY outlets that most decorative paint is sold.

Standing back

The present chapter is counterpoised to the previous one, and seeks to show that if one starts with an industry, not different countries, the different industries have their own dynamics and each of these exhibits cross-border regularities. One can in fact go a little further. Even on the modest base of the four industries reviewed here there are some themes that are cross-industry and cross-country.

The most obvious of these is concentration, which is common to all four industries, albeit with different motivations: sometimes concentration takes place in order to gain access to new markets, sometimes to amortise heavy R&D expenditure through increased sales, sometimes to achieve greater economies of scale, and so on. It will be remembered that concentration in the 1980s and 1990s was a common theme among the executives from four different industries whose testimony was cited earlier in connection with the impact of the Single European Market.

Then there is the balance of power shift from manufacturing to retail, affirmed by representatives of three of the four industries discussed in the present chapter. It is worth pointing out that there are a number of dimensions to this relative growth in retail power:

- Concentration of retailers, parallel to concentration in manufacturing, produces larger retail entities with greater buying power.
- The desire of retail chains or 'multiples' to offer own-label versions of products at a lower price than the manufacturers' branded versions.
- The desire of the multiples to simplify the product ranges they carry, thus making a decision on behalf of manufacturers that the manufacturers themselves used to make.
- Similarly a desire by the multiples to simplify the supply structure, that is, to buy larger quantities from a smaller number of suppliers;

this in turn makes each retail buying decision more crucial for the suppliers.
- The geographical extension within Europe of retail influence; for example the setting up DIY chains in Southern Europe.

It may well be that the relative growth in retail power will come to be viewed as a key change in business in the late twentieth century.

Finally there is the question of the omnipresence of change, even if the change stimuli are different for the four different industries. The significance of this should not be overlooked. After all these four industries are not high-tech, cutting-edge affairs: cables, shoes, paint and chocolates are all rather traditional and certainly not new. But they variously face change stimuli from:

- Health and environmental pressures.
- Retailer power, as outlined above.
- Changing customer demand, not just for lower prices, but for product innovation, different 'recipes', systems rather than artefacts and so on.
- Changes in the structure of markets/customers.
- The merging of traditionally separate industries, for example chocolate and biscuits, petroleum and paint.
- The decline or saturation of some traditional markets and the opening up of new ones, for instance Eastern Europe, the richer parts of Asia, and Latin America.

Europe: continent introuvable

In three successive chapters we have confronted the question of the tension in Europe between the forces of homogenisation and the continuation of diversity. We have done so because Europe represents a continent *par excellence* for the analysis of such tension.

Consider that an ever growing number of European countries have allied for the purposes of trade and mutual economic advancement, and at time of writing (1997) that alliance (the EU) has existed for some 40 years. Consider that the only real rival to the EU is NAFTA (the North American Free Trade Agreement), that NAFTA has existed only since 1994, that it currently consists only of three countries, that it lacks the idealistic underpinning of the EU as well as its integrational aspirations, and that since its inception the two richest founder members – Canada and the USA – have devoted most of their energy to mutual accusations of quota violation. The EU is a force for homogenisation without precedent in economic history: whether or not it is efficacious is another question.

Europe is also highly industrialised and economically advanced. While there may be differences in degree, and not only north–south differences (consider for instance how much more industrialised Sweden is compared with Norway, or Italy compared with Greece), the overall level is high. As a consequence it is a strategic site for the analysis of business trends and the probing of strategic consciousness comparable only to the USA.

At the same time Europe is also remarkable for its patchwork character. What other area of the world has so many independent nation states in so small an area and with so many common borders (Europe's central country, Germany, has borders with nine other states). What is more, where other areas are made up of a lot of separate states, they tend to be more homogeneous than the countries of Europe. So that the Middle East, for example, has a host of sovereign states but they are alike in being Muslim and Arabic speaking, even if their political systems diverge. Or again the 20 or so countries of Latin America share Hispanic colonial origins and Roman Catholicism, and all but one of them (Brazil) are Spanish speaking. What other region has the linguistic, cultural and historic diversity of Europe?

The result is that complexity is the essence. There are no cosy answers and few safe generalisations.

CHAPTER 5

Strategy as a force field

A theme in German history is the *Drang nach Osten*, the pressure to the East, which was called into play from the time of the Teutonic knights to that of Adolf Hitler. Changing the phrase a little we would like to call attention in the field of academic endeavour to a *Drang nach Ordnung*, a compulsion to impose order. Academics, confronted with the mess and complexity of the real world seek to order it in the sense of establishing rules, positing patterns of cause and effect and proclaiming typologies (the classification of types).

Drang nach Ordnung is in evidence in the classification of types of industry in an international and strategic sense. Industries, and by implication the companies in these industries, are defined predominantly along a global to local axis (Bartlett and Ghoshal, 1989). Global industries have products for which there is a world-wide demand; products such as Levi jeans, Coca-Cola, and consumer electrical good, are often cited as examples. Companies operating in global industries sell in all or most geographic markets, they thrive on the standardisation of both product and marketing mix, and on economies of scale. In global industries the same companies compete with each other in all or most markets.

At the other end of the global versus local continuum are multidomestic industries. A multidomestic industry is one in which the markets in various countries differ, so that the same product or service cannot be offered in all markets, and the products and promotional activities associated with them need to be adapted to each market. A textbook example of a multidomestic industry is washing powders, which have to be endlessly adapted to suit the different water heating capabilities of washing machines in various countries. An extreme example of a multidomestic market is newspapers. The newspapers of one country are virtually unsellable in another country, even when a language is shared. Americans do not read British newspapers; Flemish is virtually the same as Dutch, but Flemish-speaking Belgians do not read Dutch newspapers – when Belgians buy a newspaper they want to read about Belgian not Dutch politics, Belgian not Dutch sporting events, and so on. For companies operating in multidomestic industries, international strategy is the sum of the separate strategies for separate countries, since the key feature of multidomestic industries is the need for local (country-specific) responsiveness.

Running through this global versus local distinction is the idea that it is R&D costs above all that force industries to become global. If R&D costs are high then companies will seek to spread these costs over a larger market, which means they expand internationally and attempt to sell the same product in many national markets, and hence achieve economies of scale through a higher volume of production. Companies in multidomestic industries are in the opposite position to those in global industries and endlessly adapt their products for different national markets; their stock in trade is the Flemish newspaper, not the Boeing 747.

In fact these two forces – forces for global integration and for local responsiveness – may be weighted to yield four types of industry and/or internationally operating company, as shown in Figure 5.1.

However the emphasis is invariably placed on the two extreme cases:

- high pressure for global integration → global industry,
- high pressure for local responsiveness → multidomestic industry,

even if crossing the two dimensions yields the four types shown in Figure 5.1.

We would like to challenge this traditional emphasis. First, the global versus local model does not give us any indication of the unique relationship between the international dynamics of a given industry and the multinational development of a particular company. That is, the analysis may point to the existence of, for example, a global industry, but without all the companies in that industry developing global competencies and behaviours. Second, we would like to suggest that plotting the reality of an industry in terms of this global–local dimension leads to an undue emphasis on the extremes and thus to a regrettable neglect of the middle ground, that is, what we have termed mixed industries (see Figure 5.1).

While it is not difficult to find examples of global and multidomestic industries, it is questionable whether there are that many of either of these extreme types (in textbooks there is a tendency for the same examples to recur). On the other hand there are probably rather a lot of industries that are mixed. There is not much discussion in the literature of mixed industries, and there is also a tendency to view mixed industries as being transient, a lay-by on the road to global or multidomestic maturity.

Instead of following this trend of focusing on the extremes, we shall focus on mixed industries and explore their dynamics in terms of the four industries reviewed in the previous chapter to illustrate the clustering of industry issues. (The following discussion draws on a multicountry study of the international dynamics of industries, carried out under the leadership of Tugral Atamer of

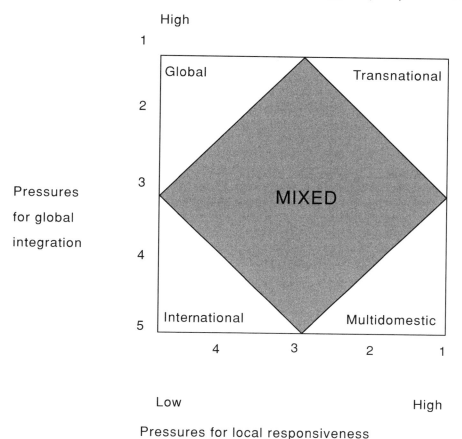

FIGURE 5.1   Types of industry by strategic orientation

ESC Lyon in France and funded by the EU; the present writer was a member of this multinational research group.)

What is mixed?

There are a number of ways in which the phenomenon of mixed industries may be identified. This may be done most obviously in terms of the two forces discussed so far and depicted in Figure 5.1, those of pressure for global integration and for local responsiveness. Thus a mixed industry is one in which these two pressures are no more than moderate, and insufficient to push the industry concerned into the global or multidomestic sphere.

It is also the case that economics offers an answer of a different kind. The phenomenon of the mixed industry may be approached in terms of exchanges, literally import/export exchanges, between countries or groups of countries. Thus if more than half of the national production of a certain product is exported and more than half of its national consumption is imported, we might reasonably infer the existence of a global industry. Conversely if less than 10 per cent of production is exported and less than 10 per cent of consumption imported we might reasonably infer the existence of a multidomestic industry, with the various national markets being served by providers local to the country concerned, whether these local providers are indigenous companies or subsidiaries of multinational companies headquartered elsewhere. In fact the four industries we intend to discuss – chocolate and confectionery, footwear, cables and paint – fall between the 10 per cent or 50 per cent parameters for the EU countries included in the study.

Yet another approach draws on the idea of segmentation, where a segment is a subset of products and/or markets. The segmentation idea was introduced in Chapter 2 in the discussion of executive perceptions of the Single European Market to suggest that companies develop strategies on a segment-by-segment basis rather than on a whole-industry basis. This segmentation is relevant to the identification of mixed industries.

To enlarge on this idea, it is both possible and meaningful to point to different segments of the four industries, as we did in Chapter 4 as part of the

TABLE 5.1   Segmentation in four industries

Industry	Segment*	Type
Confectionery	Countlines	Global
	Bars of chocolate	Mixed
	Seasonal or speciality products e.g. Easter eggs	Multidomestic
Cables	Submarine cables	Global
	Enamelled wires	Mixed
	Low-voltage copper cables	Multidomestic
Footwear	Women's luxury shoes	Global
	Leisure shoes	Mixed
	Ordinary casual shoes	Multidomestic
Paints	Industrial paints (cars, ships, aeroplanes)	Global
	Stains and varnish for wood	Mixed
	Decorative paint (for private houses)	Multidomestic

* These products are just a few examples frum a much longer list.

TABLE 5.2   Global versus local pressures in one industry

Global pressures	Local pressures
High R&D costs Downward pressure on prices Key competitors in all markets	Pressure to adapt to purchasing behaviour of customers Effect of different national norms and standards

discussion on industry issues. Furthermore these segments may be global, multidomestic or mixed, as shown in Table 5.1.

Thus the four industries that are the basis of the present discussion emerge as mixed in terms of segmentation, indeed mixed in two senses:

- Single industries have segments of different kinds – global, mixed, multidomestic.
- All four industries contain some segments that are mixed.

Finally, if we revert for a moment to the industry level of analysis we discover yet another way of understanding the phenomenon of the mixed industry. That is, industries may be mixed not just in the residual sense that global integration or local adaptation pressures are too weak to push the industry into a strong global or multidomestic sphere, but it is equally possible that strong global integration and local adaptation pressures may *coexist* without either force predominating. Consider for instance the cable industry, whose conflicting forces are depicted in Table 5.2.

Whither mixed?

The study that forms the basis of the present discussion involved interviews with senior managers of some 120 companies spread across the four industries in eight EU countries. While as suggested in the previous section we consider that the selected industries are mixed, when collecting our data and conducting the interviews we paid attention to how the executives themselves viewed their corporate world. The first thing to report is that they too mostly saw their companies as operating in mixed industries. The use of the word 'mostly' is not an oblique way of saying that only 51 per cent judged their companies to be mixed, but rather that not all the interviewees were familiar with the analytical dimensions concerned. A second and perhaps more interesting finding was that the majority of the interviewed managers did not anticipate a growth of globalisation.

It is important to point out that we are using the word globalisation here in its semitechnical sense, not as a synonym for internationalisation. So our executives were not denying the increasing salience of international trade nor the growth of other cross-border phenomena – mergers and acquisitions, cross-border strategic alliances, cross-border financing and so on – but for the most part were insisting that they did not anticipate a growth in pressure for global integration that would affect the structure of their industries on the global versus local axis. This is quite an important finding given the tendency to treat mixed industries as both a residual and a transient category. They appear to be neither.

Forces about a fulcrum

When it comes to the critical issue of the forces that pressurise companies into global integration the key factor is R&D costs (Kobrin, 1991). Perhaps R&D costs is too narrow a formulation and a term such as 'technological intensity' that would embrace both R&D spending and the cost of plant, production technology and manufacturing systems would be more appropriate. The idea, of course, is that the more expensive the manufacturing/production equipment and the higher the R&D costs, the greater the need to spread or amortise these over a larger production volume, in turn implying a globally acceptable, standardised product, offering economies of scale in production and the possibility of being sold in many geographic markets.

The study discussed above probed this issue by confronting the majority of the interviewees with a battery of propositions highlighting factors relating to global integration or local responsiveness, and requesting the interviewees to confirm or deny the validity of these propositions with regard to their own companies. This exercise and the results of the subsequent analysis confirmed the conventional wisdom concerning the importance of 'technological intensity' as a cause of global integration. This, however, is not to suggest that technological intensity is the only cause – our analysis confirmed the importance of technological intensity but threw up a number of other casual factors as well.

The first of these is marketing expenses, in the sense of the marketing costs to turnover ratio as well as the variation between countries with regard to the cost of distribution channels. The marketing expenses factor is two-edged. On the one hand it embraces the response of companies to variations between different national markets, and thereby 'underwrites' the fragmentation of the market. At the same time, as an expense, like R&D expenditure, it exerts pressure for amortisation, and is thus a factor that predisposes companies to move towards global integration if this is possible.

A further factor impacting on the global versus local nature of industries is the tendency of the state – the national government or another public authority – to intervene. It has been argued by other researchers (for example Doz, 1988) that if the state or other public authority is the major purchaser of the products of an industry, this will restrict the freedom of companies in that industry to develop in global or transnational directions (see Figure 5.1). Or again, as we have seen in Chapter 3 in the discussion of the European brewing industry, government intervention and regulation can significantly shape an industry's operations (this case was argued in Chapter 3 with particular reference to Britain). In short a national government as a customer of industry is a powerful force for local responsiveness, a phrase that seems almost inadequate in this connection!

Other factors revealed by the study to have a global versus local effect include:

- The comparative advantage enjoyed in different countries (a traditional economic theory factor), which influences the siting and concentration of a company's activities.
- Transportation costs, which clearly militate against global integration.
- Differences in business culture between countries, which again tends to have a fragmenting effect.
- The bargaining power of international buyers, which tends to be a force for globalisation; consider for instance the role of companies such as Heineken (see Chapter 3) and Coca Cola as buyers of paint for their cans.
- The life cycle of products, in the sense that the shorter the life cycle the greater the need to speed up the amortisation of costs and therefore to develop globally.

At the end of the day one probably could not use these eight factors predictively, to say on the basis of such 'givens' how global or local an industry will become, but it is nice to have the means for a fuller explanation of 'the way things are'. The fact that these factors appear and interact in endlessly variable configurations means that mixed industries, the ones 'caught in the middle', are subject to strategic diversity. Later we will attempt to illustrate this variety of strategic formulation in one industry, but at this stage it may be helpful to note that it derives not only from the complex of interacting factors but also from the variable perception of executives.

To put it another way, executives in the same industry may 'see things' somewhat differently. In the previous chapter, when discussing the clustering of issues in the same four industries we drew attention to a loose consensus on segmentation. But it is a loose consensus. Segmentation is to some extent in the eye of the (executive) beholder, and there were points at which segmentation testimonies diverged. Taking the confectionery industry as an example, pretty well every interviewee in that industry identified boxes of chocolates or boxed assortments as a segment. But some respondents were insistent that this segment had to be subdivided, distinguishing between chocolate creams, peppermint creams, truffles and pralines. When it came to boiled sweets, the British interviewees in particular wanted to extend and vary the categories.

The response among the interviewees in all four industries with regard to what they saw as distinct geographic zones, where a zone represents a group of countries, was much the same but not identical. The degree of consensus also varied somewhat between industries, being highest in paint and lowest in confectionery.

In short a cardinal feature of mixed industries would appear to be their strategic diversity, and there are both objective reasons for this and a subjective, perceptual element as well. One aspect, however, that does appear to conform to a pattern is the relationship between competitive advantage and geographic zone. That is to say, companies appear to be able to transfer competitive advantage within geographic zones with relative ease, but experience difficulty when attempting to do the same thing across geographic zones.

Chocolate and choice

It has been asserted throughout that strategic diversity is a feature of mixed industries, and we would like to give this idea more substance by looking at one of these industries – chocolate and confectionery – in more detail. The aim is to indicate the range of strategic and operating dimensions in terms of which companies in the industry may be plotted.

The 'plotting' in some instances involves choice, in other cases any choices are lost in corporate history and circumstantial flux. Generalising about all four industries Tugrul Atamer, in a report to the EU on behalf of a research team (Atamer, 1996), identified the following categories according to which individual companies might be plotted:

- Niche players versus mass market players.
- Company that produces many global brands versus company with few global brands.
- Company with narrow international product range versus company with broad international product range.
- Company whose manufacturing units are concentrated geographically versus company whose manufacturing units are dispersed geographically.
- Company that emphasises efficiency in manufacturing versus company that emphasises flexibility in manufacturing.

- Company with low price products versus company with premium price products.
- Company with foreign acquisition strategy versus company entering foreign markets via greenfield manufacturing sites.
- Company facing substantial international pressure versus company facing slight international pressure.
- Company with marginal export policy versus company engaged in aggressive international development.

The point is not that all of these represent active choices for particular companies, though this will often be the case, rather that plotting companies along these lines will indicate their strategic positioning, and that there is great variety. Remember that these categories were generated in the first place by an analytical review of over a hundred companies. Plotting according to these categories yields a range of configurations that represent a multitude of past or present choices.

The strategic diversity of mixed industries can be formulated in another way, this time with specific reference to chocolate and confectionery companies. The report to the EU (ibid.) noted that these companies had different logics of internationalisation. In fact six possibilities were identified:

- Internationalisation as a way of extending internationally the formula that had been successful on the domestic market, for example that of Mars (USA), Thorntons (Britain) and Ferrero Rocher (Italy).
- Internationalisation that uses the brand image and prestige of the country of origin to achieve a global position in a luxury segment. Godiva is a good illustration of this. Godiva was originally Belgian-owned and all production is undertaken in Brussels. The company clearly benefits from Belgium's reputation for cream and truffle chocolates, but it is now owned by Campbell's Soups of the USA.
- Internationalisation as a way of extending the scope of the business and increasing the opportunity to acquire new competencies. Jacobs Suchard, originally a German–Swiss merger, provides a good example since it is now owned by Kraft General Foods, which is in turn owned by Philip Morris, a US cigarette manufacturer that is understandably engaged in large-scale diversification.
- Internationalisation as a way of supporting a strong position in the home market: Hershey of the USA is a good example, and so are the leading Swedish confectionery companies Candelia and Cloetta (Marabou the market leader in Sweden is also owned by Philip Morris, and Fazer, also strong in Sweden, is Finnish).
- Internationalisation as a way of creating and consolidating a niche zone, for example Fazer is especially strong in the duty-free market with its boxed chocolate mints.

- Finally, internationalisation is sometimes a way of protecting the domestic position, as with George Payne in Britain.

The point is that mixed industries have a wide range of strategic choices and their strategic positioning is also wide, so there is a fascinating and comprehensive diversity among the companies in these mixed industries.

Finally we would like to give the central argument a further twist. Staying with the chocolate and confectionery industry, we would like to illustrate another element of diversity, and this concerns the way that some companies accept the preexisting dynamics of international competition and work within the system, while other companies seek to modify or even transform these dynamics.

One Anglo-American company 'plays it straight' and to good effect. According to an executive from that company, there is evidence of integrated production: 'So we may produce Product A and Product B in Germany and ship it to other members of the community [the EU], and Product C might get made in England and the same thing happens.' On the central importance of brands: 'Part of our strategy, a major plank of our strategy is global brands.' And 'We have over the last 10 years invested a lot in making our brands, our major brands, truly global.'

Then we have the logic of preemptive, multimarket presence and the threat of competitive retaliation – the following is an extract from a discussion between the company executive and the author:

Executive: I think it is believed in my company, you cannot be strong in one region and expect to remain a world player because the leverage in the other regions eventually will get to you. Do you understand what I am saying?

Author: Not quite. Take me another step. What will the leverage in the other regions do to you?

Executive: A very simple example. We could not be the world's leader in Product X in Europe and not be in the US Product X market. Because eventually the strength of the player in the US market will attack us. Well it is like thinking 10 years ago that you can be strong in France and have no presence in the UK.

We have quoted at length from this interview because it is convincing and totally orthodox at the same time. The examples quoted above were supported by other pronouncements in the course of the interview explaining the importance of efficient production, working the manufacturing assets hard in order to be able to offer decent quality products at reasonable prices. Another theme (common in the industry) was identifying emergent markets – South America, Central and Eastern Europe – and establishing a presence in them.

The whole testimony was compelling and very straight in an accepted-wisdom, text-book-style sense.

As a contrast, in terms of an inclination towards idiosyncratic reformulation, consider the following testimony from an executive of an Italian chocolate company. The company's basic strategy emerged in the following dialogue:

Executive: On the international market, if we want to survive in the competition with large companies like Nestlé that are much larger than us, we must be innovative. Therefore we must dedicate years to researching new products. When a new product is introduced it is exclusive, also in terms of technology.

Interviewer: Therefore, having low costs is not a critical factor . . .

Executive: We never base our work on costs. We work to create an innovative product in order to launch it on the market then distribute it to other larger markets. These are large, risky investments. However, that is our strategy. Innovation is fundamental.

A bold stand, but it got better. When the executive was asked about segmentation in the industry, there was none of the conventional countlines versus bars versus boxed assortments enumeration commonly offered by other interviewees:

> Our products are subdivided according to *motivations:* someone may want to enjoy a piece of chocolate for sheer pleasure, offer it to a friend during a break, or give it as a gift. If, on the other hand he wants a little something but isn't very hungry, then he can choose a snack such as our . . . that complete with snacks produced by Mars and Nestlé.

The executive's testimony on international strategy showed the same independence of mind:

> The company's international strategy is not to diversify in the classic sense, but to conquer new markets gradually with products that already exist. Therefore its goal is to introduce gradually products that are already successful in certain markets, to other parts of the world. . . . We still believe in a unique, exclusive product as the best weapon to defend our position and develop our market share.

Summary

The argument pursued in this chapter has a number of facets. First it is suggested that the dominant global versus local model is too simple to depict the reality of (many) internationally operating companies, that the forces for global integration and the forces for local responsiveness may contend with each other without either set of forces predominating. In both this sense, and by using industry-wide import–export ratios, many industries and the companies that operate in them are best regarded as mixed (see Figure 5.1).

Second, our study suggests that it is not just R&D expenditure/technological intensity that drives companies towards global integration. Instead we find that although technological intensity is the most important force there are a number of other forces, ranging from conventional economic factors (logistics, transport costs) to rather less substantial issues such as the cultural differences between countries and the impact of these differences on management style and practice.

Third, mixed industries may not simply be mixed 'in the round', but made up of segments that are variously global, local or mixed. This in turn highlights the appropriateness of a segment-level analysis, an idea that was developed in Chapter 2 while exploring executives' perceptions of the importance of the Single European Market to a different set of industries.

Fourth, and this is a central theme, we have argued that mixed industries are marked by strategic diversity, in various senses:

- One can specify a *variety* of strategic dimensions in terms of which individual companies in an industry may be plotted; these dimensions imply choice and/or constraint.
- We have noted a variable element in the strategic perceptions of senior executives in companies in the same industry, in the sense of perceived departures from the loose consensus depicted in Chapter 4, which explored the clustering of industry issues; for example there was some variation in the way individuals perceived geographic zones, defined segments or identified 'markets of opportunity'.
- Focusing on the chocolate industry, we noted that internationally operating companies may be driven by a number of 'dominant logics' (Atamer, 1996) of internationalisation.

Finally, drawing on interview data we contrasted an Italian and an Anglo-American company in the industry to underline the implicit choice between identifying dominant forces and then either playing by the rules or attempting an idiosyncratic reconfiguration, a variance that is part of the human condition.

References

Atamer, T. (1996) 'The Dynamics of International Competition in Europe: Top Managers Cognitions in Mixed Industries', final report to the EU on contract CHRXCT 93-02-93.

Bartlett, Christopher and Sumantra Ghoshal (1989) *Managing Across Borders*, London: Hutchinson Business Books.

Doz, Yves (1988) *Strategic Management in Multinational Companies*, Oxford: Pergamon Press.

Kobrin, Stephen (1991) 'An Empirical Analysis of the Determinants of Global Integration, *Strategic Management Journal*, vol. 12, pp. 17–31.

CHAPTER 6

Beyond the sea

So far the discussion of the strategies and behaviours of companies has tended to assume that these companies are established players in the international market, with on-going, cross-border operations and structures. At the same time one should remember that a feature of the 1980s and 1990s has been an increase in international activity, which implies that a number of companies have engaged in some form of international activity for the first time. These tend to be smaller companies, but not exclusively so (not every big company is a multinational).

There is a body of literature on the internationalisation process in which the dominant strand is casual and economic, seeking to divine the factors and forces that predispose companies to internationalise (for example Davidson, 1982). There is also an overlapping body of literature that seeks to typologise the internationalising process, suggesting stages through which companies pass (for example Siropolis, 1994). But there has been rather less focus on the experiences of individual companies, with the exception of a few collections of case studies, of which Jenster and Jarillo (1994) is probably the best. Feeling that it would be instructive to hear the testimonies of companies that had recently engaged in international activity for the first time, a group of us (the author, together with Valerie Anderson, Stuart Graham and Kevin Lamb, all of the Faculty of Business and Management at Nene College of Higher Education, Northampton, England) used our contacts to put together a sample of twenty or so companies where the international initiative was sufficiently recent for the managers involved to reconstruct the decisions that had led up to it, describe the experience and relativise it with the benefit of hindsight.

The sample was initially modest, though the study is ongoing and the data base is still being extended. A rather more significant limitation was the fact that the sample mainly consisted of British companies that had ventured abroad, or in one or two cases had had 'things done to them' by foreign companies in the sense of merger or acquisition. The consequence is that what came out of the study tended to show British patterns, but this can be high-lighted as we proceed.

We wanted to have some strong species of internationalisation activity to examine, and to this end we excluded from the sample companies whose *démarche* was simply to begin to export. Companies that start to export have primarily informational needs, and recurrent problems revolve around the choice of agents to represent them in foreign markets and the control of these agents (Lawrence, 1987). Instead we defined internationalisation as any of the following:

- Establishing a 'greenfield' manufacturing site abroad.
- Ditto sales office, contracts office and service centre.
- Cross-border acquisition.
- Cross-border joint venture or strategic alliance.

Chance and choice

The first thing that emerged in the discussions with the representatives of the sample companies was that their internationalisation was not always the result of discrete and proactive decisions. Quite a lot was the result of chance or inheritance, or had occurred in a rather reactive manner. Part of the reason for this were the rather fuzzy boundaries that companies often have in terms of corporate time and space. A company may be an independent entity at the time a researcher decides to include it in a sample and interview its key executives, but the company may well have been the result of merger and demerger, have been spun-off or reconfigured. Certainly for a minority of our sample this was relevant in explaining their patterns of international activity, in that a company may have inherited a site in another country, a set of sales agents, an extraterritorial presence somewhere, or had been commanded to activate such links by a (former) corporate master. But this matter of changing corporate architecture does not explain all of the circumstantial–reactive in-volvement in other countries.

Sometimes a company's presence in another country has been ordained by someone else. One of the companies, for example, wanted to become a techni-cal service provider to the Australian government and was told it would stand little chance unless it established a contracts office in Australia. Another of the companies had established itself in the Philippines simply because it had followed a large American corporate customer there. Yet another had decided to set up a greenfield manufacturing site in Germany and had chosen the location for this operation on the basis of subsidies offered by the various *Land* governments.

Nor should one underestimate the importance of pure chance. One of the companies had substantial business in Taiwan, where it was a subcontractor to a public authority. On examination this turned out to be the result of one of the company's salesmen having married a Taiwanese girl and benefiting via her family from some useful business introductions. Another's business activities in France were unmatched in the other continental European countries, simply because once upon a time a go-getting salesman had been appointed who happened to speak French. Another company needed to centralise its R&D facilities and to do so outside the UK: it chose not the countries where it had substantial business – France and Germany – but the USA, 'because we have spare office space there'. The CEO of a company in the financial services sector had decided to enter the credit card business (through corporate acquisition) on hearing, purely by chance, of the profits a rival had made by participating in a credit card operation. Yet another company had bought a controlling share in a French company in part to rescue the owner (a damsel in distress) whom they had got to know personally because 'we were suppliers to the same large retail customer in London'.

There does not seem to be much reference to factors of this kind in the literature, and of course they do not readily fit a casual mode. Also relevant here is the academic tendency to render the world more rational than it is, the *Drang nach Ordnung* referred to in the previous chapter.

Anglo-Saxon business

Back-tracking for a moment to the range of activities and developments that were counted as constituting internationalisation, a fairly strong pattern emerged in a rather limited sample of a preference for acquisition as a means of foreign market entry. There were in fact no joint ventures or strategic alliances, and greenfield sites were exceeded in number by cross-border acquisitions. This small sample had to its credit acquisitions in France, Belgium, Germany, Poland, India and the USA, with France and Germany figuring most frequently. Until we have extended this study to include a subset of newly internationalising companies in some continental European country or countries, then this inference must be tentative but we suspect that acquisition, with its overfocus on control, direction and managerial prerogative, is likely to be the British first choice, as it is the American. This view is also consistent with what might be termed the dominant coalitions in companies who take and implement internationalisation decisions.

Going shopping

We have noted that acquisition was the dominant internationalisation activity for our sample of British companies. One would expect acquisition initiatives to come from the top, but we were surprised at the limited number of decision takers involved. Typically such acquisition decisions were taken and implemented by the managing director and finance director, pretty much acting alone, or in the case of owner-managed companies, by owners with inside or outside advisors of their choice. And for these decision makers one consideration seems to have been paramount: price. What the acquisition targets have in common is that they are either being sold under duress – by a disenchanted foreign owner in a back-to-core business drive to raise revenue in order to repay loan stock – or they are simply 'going cheap' because they are performing badly. Cheapness is attractive to this particular type of buyer, when a deal-making attitude predominates. Again this may well be a British or Anglo-American phenomenon, at least to a degree.

In short acquisitions tend to be price-driven and opportunistic rather than strategic. This is not to say they are without rationale or purpose; managers describing these cross-border acquisitions may make a case for them in strategic terms, but it is often a case constructed to fit the decision. And if the acquisition turns out badly, as many do in the first instance, then whatever happens one can always claim that 'at least we got it cheap'.

An emotive dimension

But price (money) was not the only consideration. It was also quite clear from the interviews that internationalisation was seen as 'a good thing'. Smaller companies in particular saw it as a step forward, as something to be proud of, as adding to one's corporate consequence, as a stage on a broad path that might lead from humble beginnings to MNC status in the medium term. This was true of internationalisation *démarches* in general and particularly of acquisitions.

A nice example of this was the president of an American company with which one of the British companies in the sample had merged. A German company with complementary products came on to the market and the US president resolved to buy it, though it would subsequently be looked after by the British managing director, who after all was nearer to the right continent.

A very plausible case could be made for this acquisition:

- The company had a reputation for quality and technical leadership (not entirely deserved as it turned out, but that is being wise after the event).
- Its products were complementary to those of the acquiring company rather than in competition with them.
- It had agent networks in some countries where the Anglo-American company was not represented.

- It had an off-shore manufacturing entity in India, which should offer substantial cost savings.

And of course it was going cheap. But this is not the whole story. The first move was for the British managing director to inspect the German company, however he was not impressed and recommended against purchase. Then the partners employed an independent German consultant to look at the company and offer a fresh professional view. This consultant recommended against purchase as well. Then the American president sent his own account-ant to evaluate the German company: he too recommended against purchase. But the American bought it anyway!

There is a sense in which he may well have got value for money, in that the whole episode was really quite thrilling. The American liked to say afterwards how his accountant went pale on hearing they had bought the German com-pany. This company was in fact bigger than either of its masters, and the American president liked being able to talk about 'my bridgehead in mainland Europe'.

It should be added that acquisitions are exacting in a decisional sense, as well as adding to the status and substance of the acquirer. How many of us have actually bought a company, never mind one in another country?

Control

A finding that we had not anticipated was that most of the companies that had made acquisitions had problems with controlling them afterwards. This is surprising because one would think that if you buy a company, then it is yours, you can do what you like with it, and everyone will jolly well have to do what you say. However compelling this may be as a commonsense propo-sition it turns out to be flawed in practice. At the heart, most companies that are acquired do not want to be. They are mildly resentful and easily slide into the role of the unwilling army conscript who relishes nothing better than delivering bad news to the silly young lieutenant who is supposed to be in command. The employees of the acquired company also have the power of tactical response when there is a national frontier or two between them and the new owners. The latter will probably not know what French law is on this or that matter, what the German regulations are, what Swedish legislation has to say about worker representation, or who needs to be bribed in such and such a country.

We had an excellent chance to observe this phenomenon in reverse with regard to a British company that had been taken over by an Australian com-pany, both of which operated in an industry that was subject to a high degree of regulation. One sensed that the British management did not relish this development, but as it turned out the 'victim' came out on top since:

- The British product range found more favour in Australia than vice versa.
- Pre-acquisition the Australian company had a skeletal branch network in Britain, but the acquisition rendered this superfluous and it was closed.
- Regulatory complications made it difficult for the Australians to direct the British.
- The Australian company was interested in using the British company as a springboard to continental European markets, but it did not have any experience of these markets and had to depend on British advice.

The importance of the last point should not be underestimated. It is akin to the eighteenth-century Prime Minister Robert Walpole telling the German-speaking King George I in Latin what the House of Commons had debated in English, and what in consequence was and was not possible. A manager of the British company, reviewing the post-acquisition developments, observed that 'It was more like a partnership than a takeover.'

One could see the same sorts of thing happening to the British companies in the survey after they had made acquisitions, although the processes were not always so transparent. One of the British companies, a semidiversified conglomerate with a lot of domestic acquisition experience, had bought a similar company in France. We were told that the French CEO would not 'let' the British executives go round the company they had just bought unless he accompanied them. Another company had bought a similar company in Belgium, and the finance director of the British company complained that the Belgian boss would not let him talk to his opposite number in Belgium. Testimonies of this kind were common, but for reasons that probably have to be experienced to be understood, the acquirers tend not to force the issue. It is also clear that it can be more than a matter of restricted access to plant or information. The German company acquired by the Anglo-American partnership discussed in the previous section is a splendid example of this phenomenon in action.

In this instance the Germans proved themselves masters of non-compliance. Before the acquisition the German company had suffered declining sales revenues and had tried to counter this with a series of price rises. Post-acquisition it was ordered not to raise prices again. It raised them. It was told to produce a new catalogue to promote sales on a wider scale, including in the UK. It reprinted the old catalogue (which included some discontinued product lines), claiming that this had saved money on printing. It was ordered to ship products direct from its Indian subsidiary to Britain for resale. It carried on shipping these products to Germany, and then passing them on to

Britain at a marked-up price: the explanation given was that only the Germans had the sophisticated equipment to do the final presales testing. Exasperated, the American president made a personal visit to the German subsidiary, read the riot act, picked out some likely henchmen, gave them 'battlefield promotion' and instructed them on how to sort things out. Returning three months later the American found nothing had changed, his hand-picked 'change agents' coyly indicated that before they could act they needed new job descriptions and their new status had to be confirmed by the *Betriebsrat* (works council).

We noted above that internationalisation decisions seem to be taken by just one or two people, or at most by a small group at the top. One implication of this is that there is seldom a personnel or HRM (human resource management) input into the decision. This is not because the companies in our sample were too small to have separate personnel departments and managers, most of them did, but the personnel managers did not seem to have been involved in planning such moves or indeed in anticipating their consequences.

This is a pity since both employee legislation and labour markets differ from country to country. Those companies making acquisitions, and even more those engaged in establishing greenfield manufacturing sites in another country, could not always anticipate the ease or difficulty they would experience in acquiring the kinds of (foreign) employee their operations needed. As one British managing director who had established a new manufacturing operation in Germany put it 'In Britain I pay £35000 for a good salesman, in Germany it is £65000 – and I have to give him a BMW.' In addition, a lot of recruitment of new employees at home takes place via informal contact, or more formally via the internal labour market. Neither of these phenomena are absent in other countries, they are just more difficult to access.

At time of writing (1997) Britain does not have a system of codetermination or industrial democracy, but many of the Continental European countries do have such systems, and this represents a contingency for those who wish to buy or invest in mainland Europe. It should be noted that Germany in particular has a multilevel, long-established industrial democracy system and there is no way of avoiding that system – each and every place of work that employs five or more people has to have a *Betriebsrat* or works council. And of course several of the companies in our sample were understandably attracted to Germany as Europe's largest market.

The managers of the British companies in our sample did not rail against continental European industrial democracy, although Americans frequently do (Lawrence, 1996). But some of them did seem to have been taken by surprise by it. As the representative of a company that had invested in France put it: 'And then we discovered this thing called the *comité d'entreprise*.'

It would appear from our sample that companies making cross-border acquisitions often find that they want to downsize after doing so, but the rules on employee compensation are quite stringent in some of the continental

European countries. One of the companies in our sample had bought a French company in the same industry, only to find that the company was supplying a different market from its British parent, and furthermore this market was in decline. It responded by reducing the workforce in its new French subsidiary but had to pay out what it saw as enormous sums in severance pay. As a consequence the company made a loss for several years. Anther company with an acquisition in Belgium felt the need to replace one or two key staff, but it too found that this was a far from easy matter. As one representative of the British parent company put it: 'You would not guess how much it costs to make an accountant redundant in Belgium.'

The 'people issues' are not always as tangible as this, and there were instances in the sample when socio-cultural or mentality differences had impacted on a company's ability to manage its operations in another country. Such differences between countries or societies may of course be reinforced by differences between political systems. The collapse of European communism, discussed in later chapters, has had exactly this effect, where Central and Eastern-European countries have been opened up to Western investment and initiatives but without an instant change of attitude on the part of managers and workers.

A company in our sample that had made an acquisition in Poland found a strange difference between managers and workers. Even though it had a medium-term need to downsize, which must have been apparent to the workforce, the latter remained very positive, ardent in their support of and desire for training in the new working practices. The managers, on the other hand, who naturally had been educated and appointed during the communist period, were more suspicious and resentful. They seemed to be primarily concerned with safeguarding their status, and did this by taking refuge in the minutiae of controls and bureaucracy. This was all very much counter to the British parent company's espoused corporate culture of openness, free communication and organisational informality.

Anticipation

There is a Christmas cracker type of joke to the effect that if you want to be absolutely safe in life you should not do anything for the first time! This aphorism is relevant to companies venturing abroad, and it raises the question of anticipation. That is to say, it invites those involved to consider in what ways the foreign environment may be different, and indeed how the internationalisation process may confront them with contingencies outwith their domestic experience. This is not always an easy task. Part of the problem is that you don't know what you don't know! Consider the case of one of the surveyed companies, which had opened a manufacturing site in Germany to service the German market.

It was clear at the outset that many areas in Germany would offer them a financial inducement to set up a factory there, and this of course was seen as a plus, something that would sway the choice between France and Germany, both of which were seen as offering very substantial markets for the company's products. But as events unfolded in Germany it became clear that these financial inducements were not an unqualified plus. As the chairman of the company observed: 'The generous aid package meant we did things we would certainly not have done on our own. For instance the Germans take a long-term perspective, meaning you are under pressure to buy not rent. We just seemed to get sucked into all this.'

The company's business was fresh food products, their customers were retailers and particularly retail chains, and the company had enjoyed massive success in Britain since its establishment in the mid 1980s. This success had been helped by trends in British retailing in the 1980s and 1990s, including retail concentration, an increase in the size of retail (supermarket) outlets, the growth of large out-of-town or edge-of-town stores, the growing logistical efficiency of distribution, and the growth of own-label products, which, other things being equal, tend to favour smaller and/or new corporate players.

Germany, it turned out, was rather different in all these respects. A strong environmental lobby had largely prevented out-of-town development, meaning there had been a proliferation of small in-town stores, which had in turn led to discounters such as Aldi and Netto engaging in price competition. There were no own-brand products and no integrated distribution systems. This consideration is critical. In the absence of own-label products the new entrant to the market is by definition in competition with established domestic brands, and has no obvious way of 'beating the system'. As the chairman put it: 'To get customers to know our product, let alone buy it, we would have had to spend large amounts on advertising.'

More was to come. The hallmark of the company's products was freshness and hence a short shelf life – six days for many of the lines. But in Germany thirty days was considered a short shelf life and six days was unheard of. According to the chairman: 'It is still part of German culture to store food for a comparatively long period. During and after the war years a whole generation of Germans learned the value of storing goods in cellars and this still has an influence on buying habits.' Added to the German consumers' lack of awareness of the benefits of fresh products was the German supermarket mentality of stock rotation and a central buying culture.

We have emphasised the problems this company had with the German operating environment precisely because Britain and Germany are in a certain sense close. Both are industrialised, North-West European parliamentary democracies, and football and beer drinking are national pastimes in both countries!

Psychic distance revisited

In cross-cultural studies the concept of psychic distance relates to the degree of perceived closeness or cultural affinity between countries, or its absence. The simple underlying idea is that a country will find it easier to relate to another country that it perceives as psychically close – that is, find it easier to understand, come to terms with and do business with.

The multicountry study that formed the basis of the two previous chapters offers some substance to this notion of psychic distance. Spain is a good example. Because of Spain's later industrialisation and its isolation in the post-Second World War period the Spanish companies in the study were often less established internationally than those of the other countries represented. In the interviews, when the Spanish executives referred to cross-border business relations, whether ongoing or projected, the reference was primarily to France, Italy and of course Portugal. That is, the Spanish thought in the first instance of other Mediterranean countries where the perceived psychic distance was small. It does not matter that Zürich was probably closer to them than Naples; the issue was that they did not feel close to Switzerland.

The opposide was true of Latin America. In virtually all of the interviews with Spanish executives there were references to connections with Latin America – the possession of markets, agents or manufacturing subsidiaries there, the existence of South American suppliers, or the possibility of mergers, acquisitions or joint ventures. Now it might be argued that this Spanish business predilection for South America reflects the fact that, apart from Brazil, all the Latin American countries are former Spanish colonies. While this is a perfectly sensible explanation it should be noted that it also embraces the notion of psychic distance (closeness), as there is shared language, ethnicity and religion.

Hence the notion of psychic distance is not only established in the literature, it is also possible to demonstrate that it is an influencial factor in business activities. On the basis of the present discussion of newly internationalising British companies, however, some qualification of the psychic distance idea seems to be in order. It did not seem to hold for the internationalising endeavours of the British companies concerned. When asked about the parts of the world in which they were getting on well, the answer was Asia. And in answer to the question of where did they had experienced the most difficulties the answer was continental Europe. But of course in terms of the psychic distance argument it should have been the other way round: Britain may be different from France but even so France should be psychically closer than Taiwan.

A partial explanation of this could be that the cultural differences between countries are subtle and intriguing and cannot be approached directly as though they are physical phenomena, and therefore they are endlessly fascinating and tend to move to centre stage. Yet for businesses venturing abroad, while these cultural differences do matter, rather more immediate is the impact of various institutional and regulatory differences. As we have seen, it is issues such as employee rights, codetermination, remuneration differentials, environmental requirements and differences in the operation of markets that most obviously affect companies. And Europe has much of all of this, both because it is made up of rich and regulated countries, and because there are a lot of them, so that in spite of the best efforts of Brussels and the EU, Europe is an institutional and regulatory mosaic. What is more this (continental) phenomenon is rather more acute when viewed from Britain. This is partly because Britain is physically separated from the continent. But also relevant is the fact that at least in business matters Britain is rather Americanised, and this distances it from the continent while at the same time furnishing it with a different frame of reference.

To return to the psychic distance theory, it is probably fair to say that to get a sharper picture of the relationship between national societies the perceptual and intangible considerations (psychic distance) need to be supplemented by the more concrete question of regulatory difference. This consideration helps to explain the apparent ease with which the companies in the sample adapted to the much more obviously distant countries of Asia. That is to say, many Asian countries have lower regulatory thresholds and thus offer less in the way of stumbling blocks to incoming businesses.

What is more people *expect* differences in far-flung places, so when differences are encountered they do not constitute a setback. While British people may well think that the Germans are 'just like us really' (at least until they buy a German company!) they certainly do not have this preconception about the people in the Philippines. There again, going to Asia may seem less daunting than going to Belgium because of the colonial heritage, which will tend to inspire in British people the conviction that Asia may be different but 'we can handle it' (perhaps even have an historic right to handle it). So the psychic distance idea, while perfectly valid, may also be subject to overriding factors. Britain seems to be adept at cultural overriding.

Reflections

Looking back over the experiences of these companies in foreign countries it is possible to identify some causes and effects. One might begin by noting that there is a failure rate: something like one in four of the companies surveyed had failed in their foreign endeavours, that is, they had encountered problems and setbacks that had adversely affected their profitability and as a consequence they had withdrawn from the venture: pulled out of a country market, resold an acquisition and so on. There is of course nothing final about what might be described as a tactical withdrawals. The companies concerned are free to try again, use a different method of market entry, and when they do they will have the benefit of experience on their side. Of the twenty or so companies in the sample, two seem to have been very successful. The remainder encountered some problems along the way, but persisted and eventually made a success of it.

Handicapped decision making

Why were problems encountered by so many of the companies? Part of the answer is that the companies and their managers were handicapped in their decision making. Many of the decisions that needed to be made would have been the same as the ones made in the domestic environment, but abroad these decisions were more problematic – one does not know how to weigh the factors, one's understanding of the context is limited, there are more unknowns and one has less 'feel' for the situation.

This is brought out very nicely in a Jenster and Jarillo (1994) case study, which describes the attempt by the owner of a Belgian furniture company to appoint a president for the newly founded US subsidiary. It came down to a choice between two candidates, both American citizens of course, whose CVs were included in the case study. These CVs posed all sorts of problems with regard to judging the suitability of the candidates in the American context. One candidate had had a series of sales and marketing jobs, while the other had held general management posts with responsibility for results. Was the first candidate qualified in American eyes for the challenge of managing a foreign-owned subsidiary: the prospective employer would know the norms for Belgium, but what about the USA? One candidate began his CV by stating his career objective: Europeans do not do this, so how was it to be interpreted? What was the relative standing of the *almer maters* – Chapel Hill, North Carolina, versus Michigan State? The CV for one candidate included the line: 'Military status: honourable discharge'. Was this a euphemism: did it mean a thrice-wounded hero or a shirker with flat feet?

Indeed personal judgements taken out of the familiar domestic context often prove tricky. In the earlier discussion of control issues we referred to a British company that had made an acquisition in France but then found that the French CEO would not let British staff visit the company unaccompanied or talk to anyone except himself. When pressed in the interview the British executive concerned said that the Frenchman had considerable presence, and was a *grande école* – educated engineer whose authority seemed to be accepted without question by the local workforce. In a situation like this it takes a lot of nerve to say 'we just bought you, so do it our way'.

Size and the unknown

When a company goes abroad it tends to be disadvantaged by size relativities, by the comparison in the foreign territory between itself and larger domestic competitors and multinational subsidiaries. One can express this differently by starting with the country of origin. A newly internationalising company is likely to be facing larger domestic rivals at home, but this disadvantage may be neutralised by greater flexibility on the part of the smaller company, by comparable know-how, by superior contacts, by pursuing niche markets in which it has comparative advantage and so on. These compensatory advantages tend to evaporate abroad, where the disadvantage of relative smallness is compounded by lack of *savoir-faire*.

An interesting variation on this theme is again offered by Jenster and Jarillo (1994). One of their case studies concerns a company in Norway that specialised in supplying retailers with fish products that included flavouring agaits. When it went abroad it could not crack the retail distribution system because of its lack of clout and profile, so it reformulated its business and specialised in the preparation of flavouring agents, which were then sold to food processors abroad rather than to retailers. In short its relative disadvantages in a foreign marketplace led it to move to a different position in the chain, becoming a supplier to manufacturers rather than a supplier of retail products.

The dynamics of anticipation

We have tried to show how difficult it is for companies going abroad to anticipate all the critical issues they will face. Indeed we tried to work through this problem with the example of the British fresh food company that set up in Germany. Tantalisingly, while at least some of the issues can be illuminated by traditional sources of information – industry analysis, market research and regulatory familiarisation – the tricky bit is knowing in the absence of experience what these issues are likely to be. There are some challenges that are unknowable and unprogrammable, that inhere in cultural and perceptual distance. It is possible to attend courses on labour law in the EU, but there are no courses for Belgians on how to interpret American CVs or on the transgenerational shaping of the German mentality by the experiences of the Second World War.

While acknowledging these very real inherent difficulties, however, it has to be said that the companies in the sample had not always done all they could. We have noted the often limited preparations for acquisitions, the restricted nature of the decision-making group, the exclusion of human resource management people from decision making, the predominance of price considerations ('at least we got it cheap') and the intrusion of emotion into what was later depicted in terms of strategic rationality. And in particular several of the companies in our sample were neglectful in the area of personnel administration. After all labour relations, employee rights and codetermination are all matters of national, legal or institutional regulation, and information is available on all of them. In short it is not an insuperable challenge to calculate in advance how much it will cost to make a Belgian accountant redundant!

There is a more general issue. While the specifics of cross-cultural differences are sometimes unprogrammable, a state of mind that anticipates the likelihood of difference will be helpful. Not all the companies had this. For some of them, everything that turned out to be different in a foreign country took them by surprise, and the range included some nasty surprises.

Old hands

Earlier we referred to two companies in the sample that had been uniformly successful in their international ventures, both by means of cross-border acquisitions. If we ask what differentiated the managers of these two companies from the rest, the answer would be that they had experience, restraint and some *savoir-faire*.

The first company is in leisure services, and its story is simply told. It made an acquisition in the Netherlands, developed it, ran it successfully for several years and resold it at a huge profit. It is now poised to do the same thing again, somewhere else. But it is considerations surrounding the core narrative that are revealing.

First, the company was the result of an MBO (management buy-out). At the time of the MBO the company was owned by a hotel chain, and before that by a music products company – both international players. Consequently the management group undertaking the MBO already had experience of international operations.

Second, the desire to go into mainland Europe was based on a simple strategic consideration: that the leisure industry market in Britain was dominated by a few big players, and therefore offered little scope for expansion to newer entrants. But in some of the continental European countries the leisure industry was much less concentrated; as the British CEO put it, there are more 'mom and pop outlets', so it was easier to break in, and easier to do so by means of acquisition. In short there was a strategic rationale and a credible means of implementing the policy – factors that were missing among some of the other companies in the sample.

Third, the prior experience seemed to introduce an element of (healthy) circumspection. The CEO's *bon mot* on companies for sale was 'If you are offered something for sale in the USA, and sometimes in mainland Europe, you can bet everyone else has looked at it first and turned it down.' And 'Internationalisation is still very much on the agenda but timing is crucial; we won't be rushed into foolish investments.'

The second company also had international experience, indeed experience of international failure, but it had learned from it. This was a commodities trading company that also had property interests. It did well at first, but got into difficulties in the late 1980s – its losses were particularly bad in the USA. It began a phased withdrawal from the businesses that had turned sour, while at the same time looking for new opportunities.

Part of the impetus came from appointing a new British managing director. This individual had an engineering background and a track record as an entrepreneur in the engineering industry. Before this appointment he had led an MBO in a British engineering company, raised money in the City, made the company effective and profitable, and then sold it at a profit. He was trusted in the City. Against the background of its earlier setbacks the company sought to capitalise on the strength of its new managing director by making acquisitions in the engineering industry. But there was more to it than this in the sense that it had a well-considered plan of what it wanted to do, *viz.*:

- To enter an industry where there were tangible assets (rather than *prima donnas* who could do amazing things, as in commodities trading).
- To avoid areas that had led to failure in the past, which would frighten investors, and to capitalise on its reconstructed senior management team's knowledge of the engineering industry.
- To go for industries with high entry barriers and industries that were fragmented (as with leisure services in continental Europe in the previous example).
- To go for companies that would offer scope for rationalisation.
- To make the first acquisition in Britain and make a success of it; this would be reassuring to investors, who would be alarmed by the prospect of a foreign adventure at an early stage.

The plan worked. They company acquired a sloppily run but cash-rich British engineering company in an uncontested, well-researched takeover, and it was able to present a convincing case to the City. On the subject of the rigorous analysis required to satisfy the City, the company secretary commented that:

'It is different when you spend your own money, there is nobody to second-guess you.' With the British acquisition successfully settled it was able to embark on a cross-border acquisition. Its target was the USA, for the following reasons:

- The company had had a lot of experience in the US market, albeit not without problems.
- It had tax losses in the USA, which were easily moveable (in the sense of being switched from one business to another) under American law.
- It was possible to gain control with a smaller shareholding in the USA.
- The company was well-connected in the USA, and this facilitated the 'shopping trip' in the sense that it was taken seriously and offered companies for sale.

In due course an American engineering company was purchased. This company was basically profitable, but had a debt-laden balance sheet that made it appear unattractive. There was a concentration of shares in the hands of a willing seller, making for a 'one-stop' purchase of effective control.

But perhaps the most interesting part of the story was the way the American acquisition was handled. Very largely the American management and systems were left in place, apart from the following:

- A few person-to-person management changes were made.
- Some changes were made to the company structure, with several small units being amalgamated into larger ones.
- Two versions of a product manufactured in the Illinois plant were also being made in a plant in Texas; this was rationalised.
- The main plant in Illinois was old and had a satellite plant in Ontario, Canada; the Illinois plant was relocated and the Canadian offshoot absorbed.
- The treasury operation (investment of the company's fluctuating surpluses and foreign currency operations) of the American company was moved to London.
- The executive bonus scheme was considered too short term and was modified.

The new British owners gave the heads of the manufacturing divisions of the American company three-year targets to supplement the existing one-year targets. These three-year targets embraced particular rationalisation projects, cash management objectives (that is, husbanding cash, building up reserves over time) and the objective of increasing overseas sales as a proportion of turnover.

The *leitmotiv* throughout this account is precautionary restraint and the necessity to proceed from a well-reasoned position.

Estimating the pay-off

In rehearsing their internationalisation initiatives the managers interviewed in the study spoke primarily in terms of the tangible and calculable – market share, yield, profitability levels, gains through rationalisation and so on. This of course was entirely rational, but it may also have represented an incomplete estimation of the benefits. When we invited the managers in the study to look back on their internationalisation ventures and draw up a balance sheet for us, some rather less predictable and sometimes less tangible gains were proffered. These included:

- A number of design and product innovations had been acquired when the overseas companies had been purchased.
- A rise in the company's standing in the industry as a result of a foreign venture or takeover.
- The foreign venture had resulted in a larger or more complete product range, which in turn had led to new sales outlets not originally anticipated.
- The acquisition of alternative sources of supply as a result of being established in a foreign country.
- Gains in management learning and development.
- Enhanced credibility with investors.

Business is construed in rational terms. That which is predictable will always have centre stage. But in the same way that some of the problems of cross-border ventures are difficult to foresee, so are some of the gains.

References

Davidson, W. (1982) *Global Strategic Management*, New York: Wiley.
Jenster, Per V. and J. Carlos Jarillo (1994) *Internationalising the Medium-Sized Firm* Copenhagen: Handelshøjskolens Forlag.
Lawrence, Peter (1987) 'The Dynamics of Exporting: The Experiences of Some British Companies', *Export*, vol. 50, no. 9, pp. 31–4.
Lawrence, Peter (1996) *Management in the USA*, London: Sage.
Siropolis, N. (1994) *Small Business Management*, Boston: Houghton Miffin.

CHAPTER 7

Eastern Europe: patterns of the past

Many people in Western Europe had a remarkable drive to work on the morning of Friday 10 November 1989. They heard on their car radios that the Berlin Wall had been opened the night before, that thousands of jubilant East Germans had passed into West Berlin. There were scenes of rejoicing at the Brandenburg Gate, champagne corks popped, cars hooted as they drove in slow procession down the West Berlin Kurfürstendam. Within weeks other communist regimes in Eastern Europe collapsed, and within eighteen months the former USSR itself broke up, and its twin military and economic arms – the Warsaw Pact and Comecon – were disbanded.

This and the two following chapters are about some of the issues engendered by these events. It is not really about prediction or advice, about saying what will happen next or what the emergent capitalist states ought to do, though there is inevitably some element of this in contemporary discussions of the region. It is about formulation, about identifying issues, about modes of interpretation.

Islands in a stream

John Donne's aphorism that no man is an island also applies to countries and their business systems. These systems are not sealed off, but are embedded in the flux of time and space. So let us pause for a moment and pose the question: does the history of Central and Eastern Europe differentiate that region in any interesting way from Western Europe?

The German historian Leopold von Ranke famously depicted Germany as *die verspätete Nation*, the belated nation, achieving statehood only in the second half of the nineteenth century. There is a touch of this about Central and

Eastern Europe. First of all, things seemed to happen a little bit later in this region. First Christianisation and then urbanisation, and later on defeudalisation, industrialisation and democratisation all seemed to lag a bit behind the West. So the region evolved with a mild inferiority complex *vis-à-vis* Western Europe.

Second, the region is haunted by the disjunction between nationality and citizenship. In the neat nation states of the West it is taken for granted that nationality and citizenship are coterminous – if your first language is Swedish, for example, you will probably live in a country called Sweden, and just about everyone whose mother tongue is Swedish will live there, and there will not be any serious anomalies, such as an enclave of Swedish speakers in Portugal yearning to be united with their linguistic kinsmen! Central and Eastern Europe have never been like this. For centuries different nationalities and language groups have been part of multicountry empires – Ottoman, Hapsburg, Tsarist. When independent states did emerge, for example Yugoslavia at the end of the First World War (1914–18), they were compromise structures, made up of several different linguistic–cultural subunits. A variation on this theme was the (belated) creation of independent states with major heterogeneous subsections, for example Czechoslovakia in 1919. Here the majority were Czechs, but a substantial minority of Slovaks were concentrated at one end of the country, spoke a slightly different language and certainly felt themselves to be different.

Third, this region, and especially the key countries of Central Europe, had come to espouse a qualitatively different middle class by the twentieth century. At the lower educational level many of the Central and East European states, for example Poland and Slovakia, did rather less well than their North and West European counterparts and displayed rather high rates of illiteracy. Yet these same states tended to have abundant provision of *higher* education and produced their own luminaries. This, combined with relatively weak industrialisation (except in Czechoslovakia) meant the predominance of a diploma-based middle class rather than property-based middle class, or one that was distinguished by its entrepreneurialism. As Wandycz (1992, p. 214) put it:

> East Central Europe could boast doctors, lawyers, engineers, scholars, and intellectuals who were second to none in Europe. None the less a gap, least visible in Czechoslovakia, between cultural aspirations and the means to satisfy them was characteristic of the entire region. . . . The fact that membership in the elite (the intelligentsia) was determined by educational standards rather than by economic status . . . symbolised the difference between East Central and Western Europe.

To this litany of belatedness – the divergence of nationality and citizenship and the propagation of an intellect-based rather than a property-based middle class – must be added the fact of discontinuity. The history of Central and

Eastern Europe shows a lack of straight forward progression. The Hapsburg and Turkish Empires blossomed and then faded away; and the Russian Empire transmogrified from Tsarist to Soviet. It was the same with individual countries. Poland, which had existed for a thousand years, was partitioned out of existence in the late eighteenth century by the surrounding great powers of the time – Austria, Prussia and Russia – only to be recreated by the Great Powers over a hundred years later at the end of the First World War. Then Poland was invaded first by Nazi Germany and a couple of weeks later by Soviet Russia at the beginning of the Second World War (1939–45). In 1945 it lost around a third of its prewar territory to the USSR, but compensated by taking a large slice of territory in the West from a defeated Germany, thus shifting the country westwards on the map.

It may well be that Poland is an extreme case in this idea of discontinuity, but the thesis does hold at a more general level. Consider that traditionally Central and Eastern Europe were more or less an extension of the West. But in 1945, when the area came under the ideological and military dominance of the former USSR, this situation was reversed. Central and Eastern Europe became a separate bloc from the West and differentiated from it in every conceivable way. Then in the wake of the events of 1989–91 the whole region experienced an about-face, and this collection of states became aspirant members of the Western capitalist community. By any standards it is a strange story.

National differences depressed by communism

The previous section briefly outlined some historical commonalties of the Central and Eastern European region that set it apart from Western Europe, but it is also important to recognise the differences between the countries in the region, differences that ware obscured during the communist period.

Precisely because communism was at one and the same time an ideology, a political system and an economic system its influence lay heavily on the states within its thrall, seemingly uniting them in a blanket of uniformity. Furthermore most of the European communist states were dominated by the USSR as members of Comecon (the economic federation of communist states) and the Warsaw Pact (a military alliance counterpoised to NATO). Added to this is the fact that the people of these states also suffered the same dreary conditions in day-to-day life – shortages, restrictions, petty oppression and the denial of individuality – so the area of Central and Eastern Europe seemed extremely homogeneous.

But this was a perceptual homogeneity, stronger in the eyes of the West than in the hearts of the East. For the West this area was 'all communist', shut off behind the Iron Curtain, really not part of the world economic system. The West saw a set of economically obscurantist countries, trading primarily with each other in non-convertible currencies at non-market prices, in the most part for shoddy goods that could not be sold in the West. But this characterisation took no account of the differences between the countries, and it is worth drawing attention to some of them here.

Let us start with language. Not only are different languages spoken in the region, but these languages fall into different linguistic groups. Certainly the Slavonic languages predominate in the area, including Russian, Ukrainian, Polish, Czech, Slovak and Bulgarian, but Romanian is a Romance language, probably closer to Italian than to any other language spoken in the East; Hungarian and Estonian belong to the Fino-Ugrian group, closer to Finnish than to any Slavonic language; and of course the people of the German Democratic Republic spoke German, more or less the same German as in West Germany.

Then of course the countries had different histories. If we take just one aspect of this – the time at which some of these states became independent – then:

- Russia had existed for over 1000 years.
- Romania and Bulgaria emerged in the nineteenth century.
- The foundation of the separate and independent states of Hungary and Czechoslovakia, and the reconstruction of Poland, took place in 1919.
- The German Democratic Republic was officially established in 1949.
- Slovakia seceded from post-communist Czechoslovakia in 1993.

This is very far from a confirmation of homogeneity. Likewise consider what happened to these countries during the Second World War (1939–45):

- The USSR, Poland, Czechoslovakia and Yugoslavia were all victims of Nazi Germany.
- Hungary was Nazi Germany's ally.
- Lithuania, Latvia and Estonia were overrun first by the USSR (1939), then by Nazi Germany (1941) and then by the USSR again (1944).
- Romania fought on both sides!

These countries also had different experiences of communism. The USSR turned to communism in 1917, whereas its satellites only became *de facto* communist in 1945. The citizens of the USSR never rebelled against the system, but those of Hungary did, in 1956. While some ten years or so of oppression followed the Hungarian uprising, this was followed by a period of liberalisation, especially economic liberalisation in the form of the famous 'goulash communism'. And remember it was Hungary that opened that country's border with Austria in the summer of 1989.

Compared with Hungary the German Democratic Republic and Romania were always 'hard line', as was Czechoslovakia, apart from during the famous Prague Spring of 1968, when a quasi-parliamentary, anti-Russia opposition emerged but foundered on implacable Russian resistance. Poland was a far cry from 'communist respectable' East Germany and Czechoslovakia. Poland was always unruly, always difficult to govern, a state where aspirations of grandeur and freedom were implicitly aided by the Roman Catholic Church. Indeed so threatening did the Polish Solidarity movement appear to its communist neighbours that they tried to insulate themselves, with Czechoslovakia taking the lead and closing its border with Poland in 1981.

Differences under communism

Communism may have made the countries of Central and Eastern Europe seem more alike, repressed their differences (the metaphor of the straightjacket is not an unreasonable one), but even from an economic standpoint there were some differences among these states during the communist period, some of them actually facilitated by the system. The satellite countries varied greatly in their level of precommunist industrialisation, two of them – the German Democratic Republic (GDR) and Czechoslovakia – having been highly industrialised before the Second World War (Czechoslovakia, incidentally, was one of the world's 20 richest states in 1939). Consequently rather more was expected of these two countries during the communist period, and they were principal exporters of manufactured goods to the other Comecon countries. Correspondingly the USSR was a prime supplier of raw materials, especially oil and natural gas. Furthermore there was some element of planned, rational specialisation within the Comecon system: Hungary produced buses for all the Comecon countries, a lot of the heavy armaments for the Warsaw Pact armies were produced in Slovakia, and so on.

But more important than these elements of national specialisation, as planned or permitted by the communist system, was the increasing divergence of the communist states in the matter of permitting some development of a private sector. Table 7.1 shows the position for the main European communist countries, with some Western comparisons.

While these figures clearly highlight the East–West contrast, the differences among the communist countries are interesting, and in some cases striking. Czechoslovakia and Hungary had a common border but divergent economies: 3 per cent of the economy in private hands in the former and 35 per cent in the latter, and this under the straightjacket of communism.

TABLE 7.1   Share of state sector in value added

	Year	Per cent
Czechoslovakia	1989	97.0
GDR	1982	96.5
USSR	1985	96.0
Poland	1985	81.5
China	1984	73.6
Hungary	1984	65.2
France	1992	16.5
Italy	1982	14.0
West Germany	1982	10.7
UK	1983	10.7
USA	1983	1.3

Source: B. Milanovic (1990) *Privatization in Post-Communist Society*, World Bank, Washington, DC.

National character and the communist state

Since 1989–91 the world's attention has focused on the former communist states of Central and Eastern Europe, on their plight and on their liberation, their prospects and their development. However this well-meaning and very natural interest carries with it the perception of homogeneity discussed in the previous sections: the region is treated as though it has a single past, a communist past. Furthermore it is treated as though it has no future other than faltering progress towards Western capitalism. The present chapter has tried to redress the balance a little. We have argued that these states had different precommunist histories, that although the region has some commonalties that mark it off from Western Europe, there are differences between the countries, differences during and after communism.

In this spirit of squaring up to the untidy reality of Eastern Europe there is another problem of interpretation that has to be faced: it is often quite difficult to separate the effects of national culture from the effects of the communist system. Take the former USSR as an example. At a conference in the mid 1990s on developments in Central and Eastern Europe (CREEB, 1995; CREEB stands for Centre for Research on East European Business – it designates a research centre and a series of conferences starting in 1995) a British speaker with a great deal of business experience in the USSR told a fascinated audience what the Russians were like to do business with. This speaker's characterisation of the Russians included the following:

- They display a mixture of sophistication and naivety.
- They have a greater respect for *Technik* (the technical, engineering dimension).

- They like theory, but will apply it uncritically; they have high standards in education but are weak on praxis.
- In their minds, big equals good.
- They tend to think of investment as good in its own right; they have little understanding of return on investment.
- They fall for the strong American sales pitch quoting big numbers, but are unimpressed by the more restrained British style of presentation.
- They are stoical, fatalistic, lacking in curiosity, inclined to postpone things.
- They are poor at distinguishing between the past and the present, and between dreams and reality.
- Russian managers tend to issue orders and assume (wrongly) that these will be automatically executed.
- They are proud; and they may put their hearts before their heads, or cut off their noses to spite their faces.

Now this characterisation may not be right in all respects, but it is clearly based on knowledge and is consistent. And of course it raises a key question: are these behaviours and predispositions essentially Russian or essentially communist? The beguiling thing about this question is that it is simply not answerable. The only bits of the characterisation that have a communist flavour are those relating to return on investment and possibly the veneration of theory (dialectical materialism). To put it another way, think of say, Dostoevsky's novels: is there any overlap between the insights they offer into the Russian psyche and the succinct characterisation above?

The old regime

Before examining the post 1989–91 changes we need to look at their backdrop. What was the nature of the economic regime of communist Eastern Europe? This is a difficult question to answer, as suggested in the previous sections, partly because of the differences between the countries and partly because of changes over time within the communist economic system itself.

On the other hand, although this system was largely a closed one, existing behind the iron curtain, a lot of it is surprisingly well-documented. For at least some of the countries the documentation is an own-language description of the system and its rationale. This is not for the most part an exciting literature, but it does give one an official *point de départ*. Rather more exciting are accounts produced by informed outsiders. These are likely to be critical without being condemnatory. Unlike the official literature they offer 'a warts and all' portrait of the shortcomings of the system and of adjustments and responses to these shortcomings.

The former USSR is particularly well-served in this way, no doubt a side effect of the Cold War and its legacy and the desire of the USA to gather systematic information concerning its one-time European enemy. David Granick, a well-known writer on management in other countries, is the author of three books wholly or partly about business and management in the former USSR (Granick, 1955, 1960, 1972). At a later date Paul Lawrence and his coauthors produced some matched case studies of company decision making in the USA and USSR (Lawrence *et al.*, 1990). But in my view the best work is Joseph Berliner's classic study of management and factory organisation in the USSR in the 1950s (Berliner, 1957). Berliner's magnificent study is based on painstaking interviews and debriefing exercises with Russian managers who came to the West. There can be no areas of subterfuge, manipulation and the workings of the Soviet system that Berliner did not manage to uncover!

Enterprise passivity

The communist states were centrally planned or command economies. This meant that all industrial policy, objectives and output decisions were taken at government level, and that 'companies' were at the receiving end of production quotas handed down to them by a higher authority. Their task was simply to fulfil these quotas. The nearest approach to the companies and free enterprises of the West were state enterprises and manufacturing units, but they differed significantly from their Western counterparts in their passivity, in the fact that they decided little but put all their energy into responding to the objectives and output decisions taken at a higher level. It may be helpful to elaborate on this a little.

Companies in the West have to take strategic decisions in order to match their resources and capabilities to their objectives. Firms in the former command economies did not. Companies in the West decide in what product markets they wish to operate. Firms in command economies did not. Companies in the West decide how much they want to produce. Companies in command economies did not. Companies in the West have to sell the goods and services they produce, and in some cases have to establish and maintain distribution systems for these goods. Firms in command economies did not have to do this as demand usually outstripped supply – it was more a question of allocation than of selling, and the government was responsible for allocation. In the event that firms in the communist countries were producing goods for export to the West, these export sales and negotiations were handled by a foreign trade ministry external to the producing firms. For firms in these countries the customer was typically the government. The government had to be satisfied, placated and feared – but no one else did. And because the government was the customer, not only was there no marketing or selling, but the government, in the guise of some or other public authority, quite literally took the product away from the factory gate.

As firms in command economies had no strategic responsibility and there was a whole range of Western-style choices and decisions that did not concern them, they had little expertise in *general* management. Top management at firm level was technically qualified and production focused. The coordinative, policy and strategic decisions expected of general management in Western companies occurred at a much higher level in the command economy system.

Spires versus pillboxes

The institutional architecture of the former command economies was different from that of the West: there was quite simply more of it! There were more levels and linkages, more segregation, more vertical integration, and the manufacturing units at the bottom were larger than their Western equivalents.

First of all, in the communist scheme of things big meant beautiful. The communist ideal was one enormous factory, ideally (but not actually) achieving stupendous economies of scale, making goods for the whole of Comecon. Rather less clear is where the communist enthusiasm for large manufacturing units came from. It was most probably a result of presumed economic rationality fuelled by the fact that the system was driven by one very big country, the USSR, locked in postwar rivalry with another big country, the USA, which had excelled in mass production (Lawrence, 1996). Firms in communist Europe were large by Western standards, not just in the sense of the size of the workforce, but also with regard to their planned productive capacity.

Second, it was common for manufacturing units engaged in the manufacture of the same products to be administratively grouped and to report to an intermediate-level combine organisation, which in turn reported to industry ministries. The industry ministries reported to a planning commission or central planning committee, which then reported to the Politburo. In short there was a multitiered set of institutions, with information being sent upwards, and production quotas downwards, the latter typically being disaggregated at the combine level and portioned out to the relevant firms.

Third, R&D was not something that usually occurred at firm/enterprise level as in the West, but at industry level on behalf of all related enterprises. So R&D was separated from the place of production, and muct of it took place in universities and university-linked research institutes – after all in communist states the government directly controlled both higher education and productive enterprises.

Fourth, in the communist economies vertical integration went beyond the institutional tiering described above. The various inefficiencies and inflexibilites explained in the next section meant that a premium was put on securing component supplies. So whenever possible, items required for production were made in house rather than bought, and support competencies such as maintenance were located in house as well.

Thus the operations of a communist firm started further back and its institutional affiliations rose higher up. In this sense they were spires rather than pillboxes. Or to put it another way, in the communist world one would have looked in vain for companies fitting the description of 'lean, mean, fighting units', the phrase beloved by business journalists in the West in the 1980s.

Production-centred firms

Firms in the former communist states were production – centred – production was their function. The production area is where most people work, where the firm's facilities are concentrated, and it is the function in terms of whose performance the firm will be judged. It should be noted that the single criterion of performance was peculiar to the communist economies. In the West a company might be esteemed for its technical virtuosity, its record on new product development, its asset management, its marketing flair or even some strategic accomplishment, say the achievement of market dominance. In the communist economies the only question asked of a firm was whether it had met its quotas.

As a result the relative importance and status of the various departments and functions differed from those in the West. Production came first in importance but the purchasing function was vital to the communist economy. Because the allocation of components and raw materials formed part of the central plan, more effort went into predicting needs in advance. Hence purchasing departments in the former command economies were larger and had more people working in them than is the case in the West. The employees in these over-large purchasing departments were variously engaged in long-term crystal-ball gazing and short-term scrounging to try to ensure that the firm had the necessary materials to complete its production quota.

As noted earlier, sales and marketing functions were either absent or located elsewhere. R&D was also likely to be externalised, as indicated in the previous section. And the finance function had a somewhat different role from that in the West, being more concerned with post-factum justification and cosmetic recording than with Western-style planning and control.

Finally, management careers were made in and through the production function. The typical works or factory director would have been technically qualified and would have risen through a succession of production posts. There was also, of course, a requirement for political loyalty or at least political acceptability (no black marks, no contact with the West, no acts of overt opposition to the regime) for those who aspired to climb the executive ladder.

Implementation

It was suggested earlier that heads of communist firms differed from their Western counterparts in that they were responsible for implementation and not for strategy. This is not a polite way of saying that it was an easy job, that these factory directors were merely political hacks. In various ways their job was more demanding than that of their Western counterparts, required more resourcefulness, more manipulation of contacts and more nerve.

First of all production targets were set high, they were meant to be challenging. In the GDR the *anspruchsvoller Plan* reigned supreme: a production goal that was impressive, demanding and would yield a sense of achievement if attained. Joseph Berliner (1957) described how in Russia the factory directors and other managers were very strongly motivated to achieve their production targets because they carried very substantial bonuses. But if the targets were consistently attained and the bonuses paid, the targets were raised, leading to further pressure.

Second, the communist production system was inflexible. The targets were set in advance and it was difficult to have them modified. The necessary components were specified well in advance and it was easy to get it wrong; there was no free market among suppliers and the command economy firm could not threaten to take its business elsewhere, as in the West, if a supplier failed to deliver. It was common for stockists to run out of materials needed for the manufacturing programme.

Third, the manufacturing units were undercapitalised. Their plant and equipment was not the best, and certainly not the latest. These firms were unable to acquire the best, which would have to have come from the West (West Germany or the USA), as this would have been ideologically unacceptable and created hard currency problems. Even when machinery and equipment were bought from the West, in order to keep down the (hard currency) price these purchases tended to be made without an adequate purchase of spare parts. Breakdowns were common.

Fourth, firms in communist Eastern Europe functioned in an overregulated, bureaucratic and basically inefficient environment. Everything was more difficult. Whatever you needed was in short supply, you had to wait your turn, and you could get nothing without a plethora of forms and bureaucratic indentation.

All these considerations meant that the fulfilment of demanding production quotas was a real challenge. However two resources were deployed in support of production quota attainment. One of these was systematic overmanning. Productivity was low in the command economies in comparison with the West, so hard-pressed factory directors used reserves of factory labour to compensate for undercapitalisation, breakdowns and stock shortages. It was a workable solution, as after all these were socialist regimes whose ideology embraced the dignity of labour and full employment.

The other resource was human ingenuity, and particularly rule-breaking ingenuity. Managers struggled to beat the system by cannibalising machine parts (and smuggling them in from the West), putting pressure on component suppliers for favourable treatment, and wheeling and dealing within the system either to get the job done or to stage-manage the appearance of conformity. For the most part success excused infraction of the rules and unorthodox methods. But it could go wrong, and in a totalitarian regime imprisonment was a real threat, as Berliner (1957) makes clear. The precarious situation of the factory director was nicely caught by a standard expression in East Germany in the communist period: 'Der Betriebsdirektor steht immer mit einem Fuss im Gefängnis' (the factory director already has one foot in jail).

References

Berliner, Joseph (1957) *Factory Manager in the USSR*, Cambridge, Mass.: Harvard University Press.
Granick, David (1955) *Management of the Industrial Firm in the USSR: Study in Soviet Economic Planning*, New York: Columbia University Press.
Granick, David (1960) *The Red Executive: A Study of the Organization Man in Russian Industry*, New York: Doubleday.
Granick, David (1972) *Management Comparisons of Four Developed Countries: France, Britain, US, and Russia*, Cambridge, Mass.: MIT Press.
Lawrence, Paul R. and Vlachoutsicos, Charalambos A. (eds), *Behind the Factory Walls: Decision Making in Soviet and US Enterprises*, Cambridge, Mass.: Harvard Business School.
Lawrence, Peter (1996) *Management in the USA*, London: Sage.
Milanovic, B. (1990) *Privatization in Post-Communist Societies*, mimeo, Washington, DC: World Bank.
Wandycz, Piotr (1992) *The Price of Freedom*, London: Routledge.

CHAPTER 8

Eastern Europe: a time of hope?

It is normal to depict the events of 1989–91 primarily in terms of political ideology. This is entirely legitimate yet these events came to constitute one of the most sensational episodes of economic dislocation in the modern world. Communist regimes fell, the Warsaw Pact was dissolved, Comecon (or the CMEA – The Council for Mutual Economic Assistance) was disbanded and Yugoslavia and the USSR broke up into separate states.

Economically all hell was let loose. The economic order that had been powered by state authority and integrated by an alliance of communist states evaporated. It may be hard in the West to grasp what this meant. An East German manager I met at that time worked at a metal fabrication plant that supplied the *Wehrmacht* (the GDR armed forces). The morning after the opening of the Berlin Wall this plant received a phone call from the Ministry of Defence ordering it to cease all production. The *Wehrmacht* was its only customer.

The state's role as customer shrank or disappeared. Often state support was withdrawn from loss-making operations. Post-communist governments withdrew price subsidies, allowing consumer prices to rise; they also cut workforces, or encouraged new owners or custodians to do so.

Trade between these states became more precarious. Not only had the system broken down, but there was also a problem with identifying the buyers. After all in the communist world the governmental authorities had commissioned production and traded its output, but with the collapse of communism it was difficult for enterprises in one state to locate and identify the relevant authorities in another state; this problem was particularly acute in the former USSR and Yugoslavia.

The problem of interstate trade was compounded by two additional factors. The first was that in the communist period these states did not have convertible currencies, and with the end of communism the progress of these states towards convertibility was uneven and variable, with Poland in the lead.

What is more, convertibility could be a handicap when trading with states whose currency fell short of the required standard. This issue is illustrated most starkly by former East Germany. Currency union was enacted between West and East Germany in June 1990, in the run-up to German reunification. This gave the GDR, as it still was, the Deutschmark, one of the world's strongest hard currencies, at a time when most of its trading partners were ex-communist states feeling their way towards currency convertibility.

The second problem was that the USSR, as indicated in the previous chapter, had been the major supplier of raw materials to the communist world, and furthermore it had supplied its allies with commodities at prices well below the world average. But from 1991 Russia allowed these prices, particularly of oil and natural gas, to rise, thereby putting up manufacturing costs and contributing to inflation in the rest of the region.

Another consequence of the drawing back of the iron curtain was that Western companies could sell into the former communist bloc and compete with indigenous suppliers. In general these Western companies had a number of advantages including:

- Higher productivity.
- Superior quality (and even if this was not the case, it was ascribed to them).
- A positive image, one redolent of Western luxury and freedom, a powerful marketing aid for consumer goods.

A British researcher, Siobhan Bygate (1998), writing about a furniture company she visited in the Czech Republic in 1993, gives an idea of this Western competition from the viewpoint a company at the receiving end:

> Indeed the firm had received numerous visitors from abroad, especially from Germany and Austria and also from East Germany, interested in luxury products but at a price which (Czech) managers knew would not cover their overdraft. In addition these visitors had complained about inadequate quality of products and expressed interest in exporting unfinished products for finishing in Germany and Austria.

And as though this problem was not enough, Bygate added:

> Managers were aware that products from abroad were also starting to compete in the Czech market with domestic products. The [Czech] managers complained that Western European visitors viewed the Czech republic as an underdeveloped country and consequently tried to force down the price of products to a level which would not even cover the purchase of raw materials.

That is the West for you! They downprice your products, flood your market and treat you like the Third World.

In short the fall of European communism may have meant an immediate gain in terms of personal freedom, and therefore a potential gain in terms of personal fulfilment, but in the short to medium term it ushered in a host of economic problems. In the three to four years after the fall of communism the states in the region experienced lower output and per capita GDP, together with higher inflation and unemployment. For most countries the decline did not bottom out until 1993 or 1994, and it took until the second part of the decade for them to reach the output and wealth levels of the late 1980s.

The stresses of the period are perceptible in mortality figures. A 1994 UNICEF report on mortality in nine Central and Eastern European countries showed that by 1994 some 800000 more people had died than would have been the case if the 1989 death rates had continued. The worst-hit countries of those surveyed were Russia, Ukraine and countries in the south-east. The Czech and Slovak Republics were scarcely affected, and by 1993 Poland showed signs of returning to the pretransition life expectancy level (interestingly Poland was among the first countries in which the decline bottomed out). According to the report most of the extra deaths were caused by heart problems, alcohol and food poisoning, accidents, homicides and suicides. The report commented: 'Such a death toll, mainly among males aged 30–55 and across so many countries, is without precedent in peacetime' (UNICEF, 1994).

The economic dislocation referred to above has presented firms and those who manage them with a range of problems and challenges. The purpose of the present chapter is to illuminate some of these.

Privatisation

You can make a fish stew out of an aquarium, but you cannot make an aquarium out of a fish stew (old Czech proverb).

In a command economy the state owns the means of production. In a free market economy the means of production are privately owned. *Ipso facto* the first act in reconstituting a market economy must be to privatise state-owned enterprises.

It was perhaps overly pessimistic to quote the fish stew proverb above, yet it is perhaps worth remembering that large-scale privatisation – sweeping privatisation at the nation state level – had never actually been done before the states in Central and Eastern Europe turned their attention to it from 1989 on

– wards. The caution that such activities require is nicely expressed by Anne Mills, a British researcher on corporate governance in Czechoslovakia:

> History has shown that it is possible to transfer the ownership of enterprises from private to state control. Is it possible, however, to take these obsolete, state owned legacies of communism, and privatise and restructure them in such a way as to make them viable entities in a free market economy? (Mills, 1996).

Privatisation mechanisms

If the first point that one had to make was that large-scale privatisation had never been done before, the second is that it may be done in a variety of different ways. Ben-Ner (1993) suggests that five alternatives schemes exist:

- The voucher scheme, which involves transferring state property to private ownership by means of the mass distribution of shares to all eligible citizens via vouchers.
- The sale scheme, which involves the direct sale of property to private individuals or corporations.
- The financial intermediaries scheme, which involves the distribution of shares to financial intermediaries, for instance mutual funds, who then distribute the shares to citizens.
- The joint venture or foreign ownership scheme, where the state sells a significant part of its shares to foreign investors.
- Employees' ownership schemes, where there is a direct transfer of shares in state-owned firms to their employees.

It has to be said, however, that these five alternative modes of privatisation propounded by Ben-Ner are somewhat in the nature of ideal types. When one looks at the process of privatisation in any particular country, the picture is usually more complicated. Consider for example Slovenia.

Privatisation in Slovenia

In 1991 the former state of Yugoslavia began to break up. Slovenia, the province in the north-west corner of the former state, seceded and became independent after a few days' fighting. A small state (population two million), it has been enviably peaceful and relatively successful economically, certainly from its inception until the time of writing (1997). When the Slovenian government made moves to privatise the state-owned enterprises it used the voucher system, though with modifications. All citizens received a voucher, the value of which was graded according to the age of the recipient: the youngest citizens received a voucher worth 100000 Slovenian tolers, whereas for citizens over 48 the voucher was worth four times as much. As a rough guide, a typical family of four received vouchers worth nearly a million Slovenian tolers. The citizens were free to decide what to do with the vouchers. They could exchange them for shares in the company for which they worked or for shares in any of the 120 or so companies up for sale. Alternatively they could swap them for shares in investment funds (Bajec, 1996).

The privatisation law in Slovenia stipulated that 20 per cent of the shares of each company being privatised must be set aside for free distribution to its current, former and retired employees. Forty per cent of the shares could be offered via public sale or by means of an internal buyout, and the remaining forty per cent were divided between two non-state funds and investment companies, as follows:

- 10 per cent to the compensation fund.
- 10 per cent to the capital fund of the pension and disability institute.
- 20 per cent to the development fund, which sold on the share packages to investment funds, albeit in paired-down form.

We have presented the Slovenian model for three reasons. First, it illustrates the contention that Ben-Ner's models are ideal types and that the reality is more complicated. Second, it demonstrates a certain ideological stance that survived the fall of the communist regime in Yugoslavia – vouchers were issued free to citizens, employees were favoured, the financing of pension and disability provisions was attended to, and so on. Third, according to another Slovenian researcher, Marko Lah (1996), some of the consequences of these arrangements have been echoed in most of the other post-communist states.

Lah's thesis is that the privatisation arrangements have led to the existence of two distinct classes of owners/shareholders: (1) managers and employees, where the employees are likely to be guided by management, and (2) external or passive owners/shareholders, represented by various state institutes and investments funds; these external shareholders are likely to have less operational knowledge of the company, and perhaps less strategic understanding. These two groups have divergent interests in the matter of wages versus profits, and also with regard to the distribution of profits. In Lah's view the new internal shareholders, the employees, have strengthened their position in the companies. The internal shareholders are a more homogeneous group, having similar interests that counterpoise those of the external shareholders.

Privatisation and managers

It has been commonplace for unemployment rates to rise in the post-communist states. Industrial managers, who of course were a privileged class under the communist régime, have an understandable concern with job security. This concern has not attracted much interest in the West, and certainly not among Western journalists. However some Western researchers who have closely observed the unfolding events have underlined this phenomenon. For Beth Kewell (1997), a British researcher whose attention was focused on companies in Eastern Poland in the early 1990s, it is a *leitmotiv*. That is to say, she identifies this concern with managerial job protection as a pervasive force likely to shape the manoeuvres of managers in the post-communist period, and likely to guide their behaviour in the process of privatisation.

The British authority on Russian affairs, Malcolm Hill (1995), notes that Russian managers saw privatisation as an opportunity to ensure job protection and the perpetuation of management control: 'In most cases, the privatisation of large factories [in the former USSR] has led to control being retained by the previous senior management, frequently reinforced by senior management majority ownership, with the remainder of the workforce only retaining minority ownership rights.'

To take another country, the Czech Republic, Siobhan Bygate (1998) notes that managers from the former régime intervened self-interestedly in the privatisation process:

> Since the Czech Republic, as indeed the Slovak Republic, lacked closer guidelines at this time, as to the remit of managerial versus shareholding responsibility, this opened up spheres of activity for either covert power (former cadre managers exploiting their insider knowledge, lack of regulation and lack of ownership knowledge to asset strip the firm) or for overt power being used with little understanding or consultation.

Ex-communist managers wanted to maintain their power and position more than they wanted anything else.

Privatisation and the state

There was a paradox running through the privatisation initiative of the post-communist states; that is, while the point of the exercise was to take these enterprises *out of state control* and into a market situation, only the state could ordain it, initiate it, devise the process, pass the legislation and supervise the process. But on occasion the paradox went further still, in that these same states were unable to shuck off the legacy of the past, the omnipotence they had enjoyed during the communist period, and as a consequence their extensive involvement in the privatisation process was calculated to undermine its purpose. The Czech Republic provides a good example, and the processes were well-documented during Anne Mills' research in both parts of Czechoslovakia in the early 1990s (Mills, 1996).

First of all the Czechoslovakian government (the process began before the division of the state into the Czech and Slovak Republics) set up a Ministry of Privatisation, and this ministry invited proposals from interested parties for the privatisation of particular enterprises. All the these proposals were first reviewed by what was known as 'the founding ministry', that is, whichever ministry the company had reported to during the communist period. The founding ministries vetted and passed on the proposals to the Ministry of Privatisation, whose job it was to decide which companies would be included in which of the successive waves of privatisation. The Ministry of Privatisation also decided on the method of privatisation, that is, direct sale to a domestic or foreign buyer, or the use of vouchers.

Once a privatisation project had been approved the formal status of the company in question changed from state-owned to private; that is, it became a private stock company as defined by the commercial code. At that stage interim ownership was transferred to the National Property Fund (NPF). The NPF appointed the supervisory board of the company (a board made up of non-executive directors) and then organised and managed the sale of the company.

If a sale was voucher-based it ultimately drew on vouchers in the possession of Czech citizens. Unlike in Slovenia, these vouchers were not distributed free to all citizens but had to be paid for and a small fee was charged for their registration. Nonetheless they were widely available. Another interesting difference is that the vouchers were not usually traded directly for shares by the citizens who held them. Instead intermediary organisations, known as investment privatisation funds, collected vouchers from citizens, invested them in various privatisation initiatives and then issued shares to the citizens in question. A lot of these privatisation investment funds were and still are owned by banks, especially by the Czech Savings Bank, which had been preeminent during the old régime.

In short the involvement of the post-communist government in the privatisation process has been substantial. The Ministry of Privatisation, the 'founding ministries' and the National Property Fund are all state bodies, and privatisation investment funds are subject to state regulation. Indeed according to Mills (ibid., pp. 268–9) 'the government has retained and indeed extended the bureaucratic control of the privatisation process as opposed to the reduction in government intervention usually associated with the growth in free market activity'.

To this government involvement in privatisation one might add the role of the Consolidated Bank. In 1991 the government established the Konsolidacni

Banke (Consolidated Bank) to attempt to deal with the massive debts accumu-
lated by the banks in respect of former state-owned enterprises. The new bank
is meant to manage this debt in order to prevent a wave of bankruptcies
among former state-owned companies. Very commendable, no doubt, but it
means that yet another state institution is playing a determining role. Indeed
given its power to manage debt and advance investment funds the
Consolidated Bank is an important arbiter of industrial policy.

Furthermore the investment privatisation funds have promoted cross-
shareholding, that is, a German-style 'insider model' rather than an Anglo-
Saxon 'outsider model'. This is not a criticism. On the whole the insider model
has served (West) Germany well. The point is rather that one needs to be
aware of what is actually being done in Eastern Europe, and to appreciate that
for the most part it is not creating American-style free market capitalism.

Privatisation in East Germany

We shall end this review of privatisation with a quite differed example, that of
the former communist state in which the process was least complicated: the
German Democratic Republic (GDR).

After the opening of the Berlin Wall in November 1989 and before
reunification in October 1990, an organisation called the *Treuhand* was established in Berlin to sell off the GDR's thousands of state-owned enterprises.
Basically the *Treuhand* sold these enterprises to other companies, German and
foreign, though the majority were bought by West German companies. In
some cases the West German companies were repossessing some part of their
corporate empire that had been geographically located in the eastern part of
Hitler's Germany and as consequence had been sequestrated by the East
German communist régime after the Second World War. The *Treuhand* also
sold some of the companies to their existing East German managers. The
Treuhand did not in fact manage to sell everything before its operations were
wound up, and a few of the enterprises from the communist period, typically
large engineering works, turned out to be unsaleable.

In short the *Treuhand*, acting as the agent of the West German state, accom-
plished its mission in reasonable time and without the complications experienced in most of the other ex-communist states. At the same time the
operations of the *Treuhand* were little more than an exercise in rough justice.
The present author visited the former GDR a lot in the 1991–94 period and
noted a clear East German critique of the *Treuhand's* operation, which went
like this:

- The *Treuhand* was committed to making sales at all costs, and would
  sometimes sell to unsavoury buyers on unsatisfactory terms (that is,
  unsatisfactory to East Germans).

- The *Treuhand* was selling these former state-owned enterprises to raise money rather than to achieve optimum solutions for East Germany (the implicit West German reply was 'why not, reunification has nearly bankrupted us').
- The *Treuhand* sales were not informed by any idea of an industrial policy for the former GDR, but were reactive and opportunistic.
- The *Treuhand* looked with disfavour on management buyout proposals, believing all East German managers to be congenital bunglers and undesirables (whether or not the last point was true, it had a wide currency in East Germany in the early 1990s).
- The *Treuhand* was staffed by 'a horde of know-all *Wessis* [West Germans] and we don't like them!'

While we have made critical remarks both about the general dynamics of privatisation and about its substance in several post-communist states, these remarks are not meant to be condemnatory. As suggested at the outset with the fish stew proverb, privatisation in this context has never been done before. There are no blueprints, no one knows what is the right way to privatise former state-owned enterprises. Indeed in the country examples we have looked at there is clear, albeit variable, evidence of social responsibility, conscientious planning and a desire for completion, and all of this commands respect. At the same time the fact that no one knows how this privatisation should be effected does not mean we cannot evaluate the measures adopted in individual countries. This evaluation will also help us to see differences between privatisation in Eastern European in the west. The word privatisation is very familiar in the West, straightforward and readily understood. And this is especially true for British citizens, who have seen the privatisation of the state-owned gas and electricity companies and British Airways, among others. Like it or loathe it, we all know what it is and where it is meant to lead. Privatisation in Eastern Europe is not like this. It is complex and laden with latent consequences. These privatisation measures are the product of optimism and aspiration; but no one knows whether they will work or how well they will work.

Elements of change

Privatisation has clearly been a central event in the economic revolution of the post-communist states. At the same time we do not mean to suggest that privatisation is the only starting point for change, or even a necessary condition for it. This distinction becomes clearer in the case of the South-Eastern European countries, where privatisation has not proceeded at the same pace.

Consider for instance a mid-1990s study of organisational change in Bulgaria (Todeva, 1996).

In this study the researcher tackled the issue by comparing privatised and non-privatised construction companies in post-communist Bulgaria, both with each other and with a model of the former communist firm based on prior research. This yielded some instructive contrasts. With regard to strategy, for instance, the *raison d'être* of the former socialist firm was to carry out the Party's tasks; the targets of the state company (post-communist, not privatised) reflected a desire for security and continued existence; and the privatised company was profit driven. Likewise the socialist firm had no knowledge of the market; the state firm was committed to finding contracts and customers but lacked market knowledge; and the privatised firm developed market orientations and sought to identify market niches that it could exploit.

Of the above types of company it is the intermediate type, the state company, that is most interesting. The managers of these companies showed an inability to formulate a proper strategy, and reacted to changes in the economic system by reducing the scale of operations, reducing the labour force, leasing equipment and facilities, and cutting profit margins in order to land contracts. These managers were also concerned to gain social acceptance of the reforms they were attempting to implement (Todeva, 1996).

In short the message is that the end of communism does make a difference, even if the legal status of the company and its directing staff remain unchanged. There is a marked difference in the macro system and even non-privatised companies have to respond to this, however unwillingly. Yet a full-blooded Western free market orientation will only come with privatisation, if then!

A similar conclusion was reached by the present auther when tracking the development of a group of companies in the former GDR in the 1991–94 period (Edwards and Lawrence, 1994). However in this case privatisation, especially in the form of foreign acquisition, was seen as putting the coping stone on Westernisation, although the passage of time also seemed to move firms in this direction. That is, in the first instance we observed the same reactive–adaptive responses to the inception of the market economy as in Todeva's state companies. Yet with the passage of time these companies made further moves in the direction of market awareness and strategy development, even without privatisation. Thus our East German research tends to suggest a progressive management learning orientation.

Need to know?

At the time of the fall of communism there was much Western comment on the challenge that would be faced by Eastern European managers in their (presumably) fumbling attempts to operate in a Western style market system. They would, said the journalistic pundits, have no idea of what the demands of capitalism would be. They would not understand that there was no such thing as a free lunch, that profitability is a precondition of survival, that companies for the most part must operate without a captive customer base, that the struggle against competitors is a permanent state of being, that Western companies often feel themselves compelled to do quite irrational things to retain customer loyalty (engaging in novelties, manipulating demand, pseudo price-cutting) and so on. There was probably some truth in this critique, though the West may have self-importantly exaggerated the inability of Eastern Europeans to understand the ethic and dynamics of capitalism.

Instead of going down this well-beaten track we would like to suggest a slightly different approach. It helps to bring the learning needs of East European managers into focus if one recalls the structure of departments and functions in communist firms, what was missing and the fact that those departments/functions that did exist differed in purpose and activity from their Western counterparts.

Thus, for instance, the design function in a command economy focused on size and scale of production, on durability and maintenance, rather than on quality, technical excellence or customisation, and certainly not on fashionability. Second, as suggested in the previous chapter, communist firms did have purchasing departments, indeed these were more important and more generously staffed than those in the West, but their main function was the long-term prediction of raw material and component needs, plus short-term scrounging initiatives to make good official deficits and keep production going. But with the end of communism purchasing departments faced new contingencies that they were ill-prepared to handle. For instance they were not skilled in organising multiple sourcing, evaluating the offers of rival would-be suppliers or setting up JIT systems. Third, neither sales nor marketing functions existed under communism, with the exception of export marketing, which was handled by an external trade ministry quite separate from the manufacturing plants. Finally, under communism the function of the finance department was to provide a 'back covering' alibi in the event of failure to fulfil the plan.

If this formulation of functional difference seems too passive, consider some of the things that managers in communist economies were not practised in doing. They were not adept at costing exercises, at major make or buy decisions, at flexible production. Management accounting was generally underdeveloped. It was the same with strategic thinking. Under the old régime managers did not have to assess potential markets or think about maintaining entry barriers to deter competitors.

There is an East–West contrast in the ability to think in strategic terms, yet this may not be as obvious as some of the other knowledge deficits that affect the former command economy manager. In the West a lot of understanding is implicit. Western companies generally know the difference between cost leadership and differentiation even if they have not read Porter. They know that being a first mover, having market dominance and configuring the value chain of activities in a way that is difficult for other companies to imitate all confer an advantage. Thus Western managers are sometimes unaware of how much they do know, in contrast with Eastern managers, who are unaware of how much they don't know.

Management education presents a serious challenge in both East and West. Yet there is also a sense in which one should not be too serious about it. After all there is no one right answer, no authorised version, and needs keep changing. We noted earlier that old state-owned firms coexist with new privatised companies in Bulgaria. This same kind of capitalist and precapitalist corporate arrangement holds for most of the Eastern European countries, for instance as documented for Czechoslovakia by Mills (1996) and Bygate (1998). This mix, this survival of premarket orientations, including an ethic of social responsibility, precludes an 'authorised version' of management education in Eastern Europe. As Kostera has put it with regard to Poland: 'Today, mixed rules apply, political and economic rationalities co-exist, and success is defined according to "communist" as well as "capitalist" standards by different actors and shareholders' (Kostera, 1995, p. 674).

In fact one can go further. A lot of Western strictures on East European management education needs sound as though the beneficiaries are meant to be able to take over some Western corporate paragon such as IBM and run it like a good American company. But the reality is quite different. East European managers are being asked to manage a dynamic transition. It has not been done before, there are no rules, and no one really knows whether the contents of the aquarium can be reassembled from the fish stew. The ability to muddle through should not be undervalued.

References

Bajec, M. (1996) 'Slovenia towards the New Millennium', *Proceedings of the Second Annual Conference on Central and Eastern Europe: Towards the New Millennium*, The Business School, Buckinghamshire College.

Ben-Ner, A. (1993) 'Organisational Reform in Central and Eastern Europe', *Annals of Public and Cooperative Economy*, vol. 64, no. 3.

Bygate, Siobhan (1998) 'Inherited Networks, Embeddedness and Development in Corporate Governance: Companies within Post-Communist Czechoslovakia and Eastern Germany', PhD thesis, University of Loughborough.

Edwards, V. and P. Lawrence (1994) *Management Change in East Germany*, London: Routledge.

Hill, Malcolm (1995) 'Whither Mother Russia?', in Margaret Woods (ed.), *International Business*, London: Chapman & Hall.

Kewell, Beth (1997) 'Nation without State: Managers without Management', PhD thesis, University of Brunel.

Kostera, M. (1995) 'Differing Management Responses to Change in Poland', *Organisation Studies*, vol. 16, no. 4, pp. 674–97.

Lah, M. (1996) 'Privatisation and Business Interests in a transitional economy: the case of Slovenia', *Proceedings of the Second Annual Conference on Central and Eastern Europe: Towards the New Millennium*, The Business School, Buckinghamshire College.

Mills, Anne (1996) 'The Effect of the Transition from a Communist to a Market Based Economy on Enterprises in the Czech Republic', PhD thesis, University of Loughborough.

Todeva, E. (1996) 'Management Practices in the Socialist Economies: the Case of Bulgaria', *Proceedings of the Second Annual Conference on Central and Eastern Europe; Towards the New Millennium*, The Business School, Buckinghamshire College.

UNICEF (1994) 'Crisis in Mortality, Health and Nutrition', Geneva: UNICEF.

CHAPTER 9

Eastern Europe: consequences and response

As suggested already there are variations in the way companies have reacted to post-communism – variations from country to country, and in developments over time – and a contrast between companies that have been privatised and those that are still state-owned (as explored in the case of Bulgaria in the previous chapter). Perhaps the most disputed issue between contemporary researchers concerns the intensity of managerial proactivity. In this connection we have already cited a number of writers who have suggested that, in the companies they have examined in Russia, Poland and the Czech Republic, the managers' main concern was to preserve their jobs, and to this end they strove to preserve their companies, if necessary influencing or even taking control of the privatisation process. A different emphasis is offered by Edwards and Lawrence (1994) in their discussion of managers in the former GDR in the early 1990s, where managers typically took control and tried to make a success of their companies independently of the prospect of privatisation via the agency of the *Treuhand*. Similarly Edwards (1997), writing about post-communist Hungary in the mid 1990s, emphasises the quality of managerial proactivity.

Given these variations it is perhaps more prudent to speak of management responsiveness to the changed conditions of the post-communist world, rather than to presume a consistent proactivity. Another refinement that should be made at this juncture is to say that although as a matter of convenience one speaks of 'management' or 'managers', changes in the composition of management may have occurred in the early stages of the post-communist period. First of all, top managers who were overidentified with the former communist régimes may have been pushed out, and less senior managers who had the confidence of their peers may have been pushed up into the 'hot seat'. A further variation is that people who had held management positions in firm-based, party political and trade union representative structures, whose *raison d'être* had ceased with the fall of communism, moved into real company jobs, sometimes into newly created sales teams.

Despite these qualifications there have been a number of common developments at firm level in the post-communist period. First, firms were taken out of the vertical institutional tiers described in the previous chapter. Second, firms have been streamlined in the sense of closing down secondary operations, support facilities, in-house component manufacture and maintenance operations. Third, and closely related to this, firms have tended to look critically at their range of products and/or activities, and have reduced or simplified this range in order, in Western terms, to achieve greater focus.

As an example of some of these trends consider the Hungarian confectionery company Quintie (Edwards, 1997). Quintie was the leading confectionery company in communist Hungary, with 57 per cent of the market. It employed nearly 3000 people in four factories, produced 63000 tonnes of products divided among 850 product lines, including coffee. Yet as of 1991, 104 of these 850 product lines accounted for 80 per cent of sales.

What is more Quintie had been vertically integrated to a high degree even by the standards of communist Hungary. It owned its own purchasing organisation, a cherry plantation, a plant producing 'milk crumb', and some retail outlets. It also owned some unrelated businesses.

There were of course a number of problems relating to production technology, sales, marketing, brand development and computerisation. Local management's preferred option for overcoming these limitations was to sell the company to a foreign partner. To this end the state Property Agency in post-communist Hungary decided to privatise Quintie by international tender, and it was eventually bought by Stollwerck, a West German confectionery company. Stollwerck had a presence in several West European countries, had bought a chocolate company in the former GDR, built a chocolate factory in Poznan (Poland) and planned a similar venture in Russia.

Stollwerck's measures after the acquisition of Quintie are a paradigm of reconstruction. They included:

- A DM 30 million investment, mostly in the main Budapest factory; money was spent on developing new product lines, quality improvements, and packaging technology.
- Developing a sales force.
- Closing two of the original four Quintie factories, later replacing a third of the original factories with a new greenfield site plant.
- Reducing the number of product lines from 850 to 90.

A further general trend in the post-communist period has been downsizing. For a variety of reasons explored earlier, firms in the communist period were typically overmanned. Demanning was a *leitmotiv* of the post-communist period, variously initiated defensively by local management at the start of the free market period or after privatisation, or by new foreign owners. In the 1991–93 period in the former GDR, Edwards and Lawrence (1994) found workforce reductions of 40–80 per cent, both among companies being run by their original management awaiting privatisation and in companies sold by the *Treuhand*. Again Quintie, the Hungarian confectionery company, exemplifies this trend as the workforce was reduced from an initial 2880 to 750 by 1995 under Stollwerck's ownership. One example of Stollwerck's workforce reduction was the installation of robots to pack chocolate bars, which replaced a work unit of 80 people.

Privatisation has already been discussed in some detail, but it is important to add to this 'round-up' of company-level developments the fact that privatisation is not usually something that is simply 'done to' management. As we have seen for a variety of countries, managers in the post-communist period have variously tried to shape and influence the privatisation process, organise MBOs or, for instance in Slovenia and in the former USSR, arrange more broadly based employee buyouts through the aggregation of vouchers. Perhaps the commonest motive of local management is self-preservation, but there are also cases of local mangers making a strategic assessment of their firms' needs and taking a privatisation initiative on this basis. Quintie is a case in point, and examples of such strategic initiatives have been documented in the case of the former GDR (Edwards and Lawrence, 1994).

A related issue that often preoccupied managers in the early post-communist period was the problem of indebtedness. A lot of companies entered the post-communist age with debts, typically to state banks and other agencies of the old régime. Attempts by management to reduce, reschedule or better still annul these debts were a common occurrence.

However the most pervasive and recurrent developments were a set of organisational and workforce restructuring measures, including:

- The deintegration of firms from vertical institutional chains.
- The closure of subsidiary operations of the maintenance, support and component manufacture kind.
- The closure (selling-off where possible) of outlying or subsidiary manufacturing sites.
- Often some selective changes in top management at an early stage.
- Overall workforce reduction.
- Investing where possible to improve productivity, and reducing the number of blue-collar production workers.
- A reduction in the number employed in the purchasing function.
- A reduction in the number of white-collar workers, generally by means of computerisation.
- A scramble for contacts and contracts, in more successful cases giving way eventually to a viable strategy of development.

The Czech proverb quoted in Chapter 8 is probably wrong in this application, but it is still not easy to reconstitute the aquarium!

Internationalisation

Many of the former state-owned enterprises in Eastern Europe have been acquired by foreigners, typically by foreign companies. This prompts the question, what differences are experienced by these East European firms when they are acquired by a foreign company? The remarks that follow should be seen as indicating tendencies and possibilities, not as expressing absolutes. With this qualification in mind, there are several things that should be mentioned.

First of all, foreign acquisition opens up the possibility of a clash between national cultures. This phenomenon is probably most marked in Czechoslovakia, where the (West) Germans are active in joint ventures and acquisitions, but are treated with a certain reserve because of memories of the Second World War, especially by the older generation. In the former GDR more state-owned enterprises have been acquired by West German companies than by anyone else, and justifiably or not the new owners are often stigmatised as *Besserwissis* (know-alls) by their former communist cousins.

A second tendency, and a strong one, is that with international acquisitions the directive and strategic initiative passes away from local management, no matter how able management has proved itself since the fall of communism or how proactive it has been.

Third, foreign acquisition invariably means that there will be reorganisation, often going beyond the investment–demanning–productivity improvement complex described earlier in the case of Quintie. To give another example from Hungary, the insurance company AB was acquired by Aegon of the Netherlands in 1992. In an interview in 1995 we were told that changes included:

- Organisational delayering.
- The existing territorial organisation whereby the country was divided into 20 counties, each with a county director, was replaced by six regions, each of which was classed as a profit centre.
- The number of heads of department was reduced from 48 to 20, and the top management team from 9 to 4.
- Manual administration was largely replaced by computerisation.

Finally, foreign acquisition means fitting in with new plans. The acquiring company has a bigger game to play, a game that probably extends over several countries. Typically the company will have a plan and a purpose before it moves to take over a state-owned enterprise in Eastern Europe, and when the acquisition is made the acquired company will be 'fitted in' to the designs of its new master. While any acquisition has something of this flavour, a cross-border acquisition represents a stronger version of this dynamic.

Consider as a strong example of this phenomenon a pharmaceuticals company in the former GDR. During the communist period it had its own R&D capability, made all its own products, mostly in and around Berlin, was a major supplier to the East German medical system and had substantial sales in the former USSR. For nearly four years from the opening of the Berlin Wall in November 1989 it was run by the same management team that had directed it during the communist period. During the period of independence that preceded privatisation the substantial achievements of the company included the following:

- It recaptured East German markets from West German competitors.
- It availed itself of a German export credit guarantee scheme after German reunification to make massive sales to the former USSR.
- It invested in new technology from current revenue and achieved good manufacturing practice standards, and thus the potential to sell to the West.
- It conducted the usual restructuring and demanning.

Its senior managers would probably have bought the company from the *Treuhand* if they could have raised the capital, but the company was too large. In 1993 it was sold by the *Treuhand* to an Italian pharmaceuticals company. The new owner had its own R&D capability, a substantial presence in Italy and it exported to a number of Southern European countries. But most of its production was carried out in Third World countries rather than in Italy. Its interest in acquiring the East German company was to use it as a springboard for sales in Northern Europe.

After acquisition the Italian owner set up a pan-German sales force and developed a massive marketing capability at the German company's base in Berlin. It reduced production in Berlin, further reduced the blue-collar workforce and ran down the German R&D capability. The main *raison d'être* of the German company became the sale and distribution of products developed in Italy, manufactured in the Third World and sold under the German trademark.

We have told this story not so much because the outcome was disappointing to the German employees, but because it is a good example of an acquired company being fitted into the new owner's strategy. This strategy was perfectly logical and would have seemed less remarkable in the West. The operation was a business success, with satisfactory sales being achieved in Northern Europe.

Workers

One consequence of the end of communism is that the experiences of managers and workers in the manufacturing industry have diverged. As we have already noted, managers' main concern was job security, but for those whose organisations have survived and who have not fallen victim to the restructuring outlined in the previous section, being a manager has become more interesting and more rewarding. The heavy circumscription of management authority by trade union and communist party officials is a thing of the past, as is the overdetermination of the manager's role that resulted from the rigidities of central planning. For managers who have survived the fall of communism, and most have, there is more freedom, more discretion and greater responsibility. Furthermore their salaries have risen and the pay differential between managers and their subordinates has increased. In short, they have become more like Western managers.

Workers have had the opposite experience. First, there has been the fear and for many the reality of unemployment. Second there has been the loss of all or most of the welfare benefits formerly available at work – crèche facilities, medical care, dental treatment, subsidised meals, sometimes factory shops selling goods that were not readily available at ordinary retail outlets, holiday homes, subsidised sporting and recreational facilities, and so on. Third, for many, working in communist factories had been 'a bit of a skive'. Discipline was often poor, 'goofing off' was fairly easy, so-called medical absenteeism was generally tolerated, and theft of materials and goods from the plant was pretty common. These practices and this ethos could not survive for long after the demise of communism, with the ensuing drive to improve efficiency and productivity. As one interviewee put it: 'Less people, more work, the same money!'

To these basics one may add expectations associated with the fall of communism that were not always realised, or not quickly enough, and the likelihood of this was probably strongest in newly privatised firms that were acquired by Western companies. Some of these fears and frustrations are nicely caught in a mid 1990s study of workforces in Western-acquired engineering companies in Poland and the Czech Republic (Helienek, 1996).

First, the employees in the companies studied had expected a dramatic rise in their earnings that would bring them into line with manual workers in the West; they were disappointed of course, but their expectations were very real. Second these employees bemoaned the loss of welfare provision, as noted above: 'On the enterprise level the majority of employees . . . feel that the company does not care for their social and material needs. This feeling derives from the fact that after take over by western capital almost all of the social functions of former state owned socialist enterprises were cancelled' (Helienek, 1996). The employees who expressed these opinions to Emil

Helienek and his colleagues were in Warsaw and Brno (the Czech Republic's second city). Fear of unemployment was a common theme, as one would expect, as were complaints about workloads and fluctuations in the workload with unpredictable overtime requirements.

There were also complaints about lack of information and poor communication, complaints that were justifiable when one remembers the unprecedented nature of the changes occurring and the uncertainty to which they must have given rise. The question of wage differentials also surfaced in this Polish–Czech study. Indeed Helienek rightly points out that the workers had been glorified by communist ideology; only the manual worker did 'real work', and could be sufficient unto himself. Against this background the growing differential between blue-collar workers and various grades of white-collar employees was particularly hard to take.

An interesting aspect of Helienek's study is that the employees of the engineering companies were a lot more forthcoming in the interviews than in the questionnaire survey (shades of communist oppression), and the Czech workers were rather more conformist (inhibited) than their Polish counterparts. A particularly positive response in the interviews concerned training. Under communism occupational training had had a strong ideological bent and had generally been considered boring. But in firms acquired by Western companies training had taken on a new and real importance, and the employees were responding positively to this.

Finally, it should be added that for those workers who have not fallen victim to demanning initiatives, wages have generally risen – even if not as far or as fast as those concerned would have liked. To return to the example of Quintie, the Hungarian confectionery company discussed in an earlier section, the workforce may have been reduced from nearly 3000 to 750, but those who remained experienced a 50 per cent pay rise over 3–4 years (Edwards, 1997).

Business and the crime wave

The fall of communism unleashed a wave of criminal activity across Eastern Europe. This was not of course an intended consequence for those who had demonstrated against the old communist régimes, but with the benefit of hindsight it is quite easy to explain.

The old régimes were oppressive. They demanded the obedience of their citizens, who were controlled to a far greater extent than citizens of Western countries. The people were overpoliced, bureaucratically monitored, subject to surveillance and spied upon. The purpose of all this is in the minds of the rulers was to secure the political obedience of ordinary people, but it also had the side effect of repressing crime. So in the states of communist Europe crime rates were low and detection rates high. Crimes were also treated as ideological violations, not just as simple acts of immoral acquisitiveness. Add to this the fact that there was nowhere to run, no way out of the state, which was also nicely sealed off from transborder criminal initiatives of the Mafia kind.

When the communist regimes collapsed all these restraints evaporated. There was a crumbling of public authority, a period of unstructured expectation, a scramble to retain jobs and increase personal advantage, while the new capitalist ethic seemed to endorse a get-rich-quick approach to life. Fertile ground for criminal initiatives.

The explosion of crime is understandably not well-documented at the official level, but it is widely attested by ordinary citizens in the post-communist states as well by Western visitors. In the former GDR in the 1991–94 period the present author heard abundant tales of highway robbery on Autobahn 13 (which runs from Berlin to the Polish border), danger on the streets and black market scams. The newspapers were full of letters from police chiefs bewailing the fact that their officers had to use Ladas to pursue bank robbers driving BMWs.

But East European crime is by no means an East German preserve, indeed by general consensus Russia and the Ukraine are probably the most criminalised. In a discussion on FDI (foreign direct investment) in Russia, Pulonsky and Clark (1996) cite crime as a significant deterrent to FDI. These authors quote Chrystia Freeland from the *Financial Times* to the effect that:

> Mr Yum Baturin, the Russian President's senior national security advisor, said several thousand criminal gangs, employing more than 25000 people, were operating in Russia. They controlled more than 40000 enterprises. Mr Baturin estimated that corrupt government officials assisted at least a quarter of Russia's criminal gangs (Freeland, 1995).

In particular there is a fear on the part of both would-be or existing investors in Russia that once the fact and scale of their investment is known they will become the target of criminal attention. As a consequence they are disinclined to register such investments. As noted by Michelle Celarier (1995), 'Once registered anywhere, they fear being hit for extortion money by Russia's mobsters.'

The excitement of the east

The issue of criminality, which underlies most of the threats of the region, conflates with notions of danger and therefore of excitement. In a paper engagingly entitled 'Tales from the Wild East: the Exporter as Gunslinger', three British researchers report the findings of their study of British small and medium-sized enterprises engaged in trade with Russia (Edwards *et al.*, 1996).

Three interesting points emerge from this study. First, the theories of foreign market entry reviewed by the researchers do not quite capture the disorderly reality experienced by British firms in Eastern Europe in general and Russia in particular. Some of the companies reviewed in the study were pulled into Russia as a result of being approached with a request for their goods, services or participation. Others were pushed by the poor state of domestic markets during the period of recession in Britain in the early 1990s. Others had gained a knowledge of Russian markets and made useful contacts while working for another employer, and subsequently set up their own companies.

Second, it is quite clear from the interviews that for many of these British businessmen the danger was appealing. It gave to the whole experience a sense of adventure, a bit of excitement. It gave people back home something to think about: only 'real men' go to the Wild East.

Third, Eastern Europe offers a challenge in the sense that there are more unknowns, and Russia is the strongest instance of this. That is to say, there are more things that are unprogrammable, unknowable (especially in advance) and uncertain. Especially in the earlier stages the Westerner will be wondering: who will I do business with, what will their people be like, will they drink me under the table, who are the appropriate authorities, will they expect to be bribed, and so on? The possibility of danger from criminal elements may be a part of the challenge of unknowability, but it is only a part. In these senses the East is bound to keep some of its mystery and excitement into the third millennium.

Into the European Union?

Finally we would like to link these chapters on Eastern Europe to the rest of the book, which has a primarily Western focus, by asking whether Eastern European countries should be admitted to the European Union (EU). This question can be judged absolutely or comparatively. In the former case one could ask: are all the current EU member states satisfied that such and such an East European country can fulfil all the essential criteria? The use of absolute criteria may mean that it will be a long time before any of the Eastern European countries are admitted.

A rather different approach is implicit in a fascinating CEPREMAP study, which treats the issue comparatively by asking how some of the Eastern European countries currently compare with the two least-developed Western

European states to be admitted, Greece in 1981 and Portugal in 1986 (Zaman, 1996). First of all, if one takes candidate countries' per capita GDP in relation to the EU, then there is little to choose between, say, Slovenia now and Portugal in 1986 (Table 9.1).

Taking the proportion of FDI in GDP as an indicator of economic development and openness, Zaman then shows that in 1994 the Czech Republic, Poland and Hungary were streets ahead of the FDI received by Greece in 1981 and Portugal in 1986 (Table 9.2).

TABLE 9.1 GDP per capita in Portugal and Slovenia relative to the EU

		GDP/capita (ECU)
1986	EU	9044.50
	Portugal	3199.00
	EU/Portugal	2.83
1994	EU	16317.60
	Slovenia	5491.40
	EU/Slovenia	2.97

Sources: Commission Européenne, *Economie Européenne*, no. 58, Annexe Statistique (1994); IMF, *Statistiques Financières Internationales* (1996).

TABLE 9.2 Proportion of net FDI in GDP

	(FDI/GDP)*100
Greece (1981)	0.370
Portugal (1986)	0.396
Slovenia (1994)	0.790
Czech Republic (1994)	2.440
Hungary (1994)	2.780
Poland (1994)	2.025
Bulgaria	1.150
Romania	1.100
Slovakia (1994)	1.500

Sources: Commission Européenne, *Economie Européenne*, no. 58 (1994); OECD, *Etudes Economiques de l'OCDE, Portugal* (Paris: OECD, 1992); OECD, *Etudes économiques de l'OCDE, Greece* (Paris: OECD, 1995); *Financial Times*, March 25 1996, p. 3; EBRD, *Economics of Transition*, vol. 3, no. 4 (1995).

Another possibility is to compare the foreign trade (imports plus exports as a proportion of GDP) of some of the Eastern European countries, with that of Greece in 1981 and Portugal in 1986) (Table 9.3). Interestingly this puts the Czech Republic at the top, with Portugal in second place. But all the Eastern European countries listed either do better than Greece or at least bear comparison with that country.

Zaman raises another key issue. That is, he checks per capita GDP growth for Portugal before and after EU entry, again using EU data sources. The result is really quite striking (Table 9.4). Portugal did a lot better in the four years after joining the EU than in the four years prior to entry. The implication is clear that EU membership is a determinant of economic growth rather than a consequence of having achieved such growth already. If this is broadly so, can membership be decently withheld?

This interpretation is perhaps reinforced by another of Zaman's lines of inquiry, namely productivity growth in the former GDR. If there is one post-communist country that has had a forced march down the road of economic development it is clearly the former GDR, as a result first of currency union

TABLE 9.3 Percentage of foreign trade in GDP

	$[(E + I)/GDP]*100$
Greece (1981)	21.17
Portugal (1986)	35.91
Hungary	27.15
CSFR	36.20
Poland	17.64
Romania	18.47

Sources: Commission Européenne, *Economie Européenne*, no. 58 (1994); OECD, *Etudes Economiques de l'OCDE, Portugal* (Paris: OECD, 1992); OECD, *Etudes Economiques de l'OCDE, Greece* (Paris: OECD, 1995); EBRD, *Economies of Transition*, vol. 3, no. 4 (1995); Costello and Laredo, 1994; IMF, *Statistiques Financières Internationales* (Geneva: IMF, 1993).

TABLE 9.4 Portugal: GDP per capita before and after integration

	1982	1983	1984	1985	1986	1987	1988	1989	1990
GDP/capita	2530	2482	2585	2880	3199	3381	3756	4377	5012

Source: Commission Européenne, *Econommie Européenne*, no. 58, Annexe Statistique (1994).

TABLE 9.5   East Germany: labour productivity (LP) and unit labour cost (ULC) in manufacturing (West Germany = 100)

	1991	1992	1993	1994
LP	18.2	33.5	46.3	53.7
ULC	151	125	109.5	108.5

Source: Sinn, 1995.

with West Germany and then reunification in 1990. Table 9.5 shows the changes in labour productivity and unit labour cost from 1991–94.

It should be stressed that in this section I have taken some of Zaman's data and made my own inferences from it, rather than necessarily following his interpretation.

A retrospect

Looking back on the post-1989 period from the standpoint of 1997, reviewing what I think I have learned about Eastern Europe – from visits and research, from reading and conferences, and from some of my own PhD students – there are some general thoughts that may be worth recording:

- The countries of Eastern Europe are all different (a case argued in a previous chapter).
- There is no blueprint on how to manage the transition from command economy to market economy.
- The Western way is probably not the only way, and in any case there are several Western ways.

At the end of the day 'muddling through' will be at least as important as rational intentions, and any country that manages to muddle through deserves to inherit the Earth.

References

Celarier, Michelle (1995) 'Russian Risk', *Global Finance*, vol. 9 (January 1995), pp. 32–8.
Clark, B. and G. Polonsky (1996) 'FDI in Russia: problems and perceptions', *Proceedings*

of the Second Annual Conference on Central and Eastern Europe: Towards the New Millennium, The Business School, Buckinghamshire College.

Edwards, Vincent (1997) *Hungary since Communism*, London and Basingstoke: MacMillan.

Edwards, V. and P. Lawrence (1994) *Management Change in East Germany*, London: Routledge.

Edwards, V., M. Rein and A. Woods (1996) 'Tales from the Wild East: the exporter as gunslinger', *Proceedings of the Second Annual Conference on Central and Eastern Europe: Towards the New Millennium*, The Business School, Buckinghamshire College.

Freeland, Chrystia (1995) 'Organised Crime is the Real Threat: officials say criminals believed to control more than 40000 Russian Enterprises', *Financial Times*, 14 October 1995.

Helienek, E. (1996) 'Enterprise Restructuring and Personal Climate in Large Engineering Companies in Central and Eastern Europe', *Proceedings of the Second Annual Conference on Central and Eastern Europe: Towards the New Millennium*, The Business School, Buckinghamshire College.

Zaman, C. (1996) 'The European Enlargement Towards the East: How and When?', *Proceedings of the Second Annual Conference on Central and Eastern Europe: Towards the New Millennium*, The Business School, Buckinghamshire College.

of diversity

We have drawn attention to the stark contrasts that have existed on the European continent by comparing the communist East, or its legacy, with the capitalist West. In this chapter we shall compare political ideologies and economic systems, which also have a bearing on the question of whether there might be differences between countries in matters of management practice and style below the level of overarching ideologies and systems.

To formulate the question in a more open-ended way: would one expect management style and practice to be approximately the same in different countries, at least in capitalist, democratic, industrialised countries, or would one expect identifiable differences? The answer to this question seems to depend on which period is under discussion. There are three or possibly four answers, all epochally based. The first answer is that one would expect homogeneity in management practice; the second is that it is possible to demonstrate country cultures – based differences; and the third is that while there may be differences it is possible to systematise and agglomerate these. The rather more tentative fourth answer we will keep for the final chapter.

Let us begin with answer one, which is seen as having been valid for the longest time.

Presumptions of homogeneity

For most of the time that management has been a subject it has been assumed that management practice is much the same wherever it takes place. Early writers on management – for example scientific management advocate Frederick Taylor in the early 1900s and the French mining engineer turned generalising chief executive Henri Fayol, whose influential *L'Administration général et industrielle* appeared in 1916 (the definitive second edition) – wrote

119

for the world rather than simply for their fellow countrymen. There is no suggestion that Fayol's principles were meant only for France or that Taylor's analysis of motivation and incentives applied only to US steel plants. For the first seventy years or so of the twentieth century, writing about management proceeded in terms of these general and generally applicable principles, whether they were analytical or exhortatory, or the one leading to the other, and no one sought to qualify their *dicta* or recommendations, to say that it works in California but we don't know if it works in Nigeria. In particular the classical management school, of which Henri Fayol was the founder but whose contribution and influence ran well into the 1960s, dealt expressly in terms of management universals, cause and effect dynamics that transcended culture. Since this presumption of homogeneity lasted for so long it is only reasonable to ask what arguments or forces may be cited in its support.

One very basic contributory argument is a cause and effect one, as follows:

> Management takes place in companies; all companies aim to make a profit; *ipso facto* management in these companies will tend to do the same things to bring about that profitability; managers/companies who deviate from these norms will be less profitable or even unprofitable and will disappear, strengthening the norm.

This general profitability dynamic is strengthened by two more particular ones. There is a folk saying in Yorkshire that the best way to make money is to stop losing it! This is relevant to business as well as to personal finance, that is, companies are invariably concerned with cost reduction as a contribution to profitability. Indeed companies are generally concerned with efficiency in the production and distribution of goods and services, where efficiency is an economic (value for money) relationship between necessary inputs and desirable outputs. This near universal striving for efficiency and cost reduction is an important homogenising force. Other things being equal companies will do the same sorts of things to promote efficiency and cost reduction, and this will make these companies and the managers who run them more alike than unalike.

To bring this argument up to date, the theory and practice of corporate strategy is also an homogenising force. Most strategic analysis is acultural, the dynamics of competitive behaviour are thought to be universal. From Minneapolis to Bangkok, people who run companies are thinking about how to sustain competitive advantage, maintain market share and please shareholders. It is possible to have creative departures from the strategic norm, and we tried to illustrate this in Chapter 5 with reference to the European confectionery industry, but it has to be said that this is not accepted wisdom among strategy preachers and teachers. It is rather that the strategy perspective is universal, the tools of analysis are the same, and they are well-recognised levers for desired outcomes.

There is another two-step argument in favour of management homogeneity that starts with technology. The argument goes like this. There is a whole body of research that links technology and organisational structure, and shows that technology shapes work organisation. And organisational structure and work organisation in turn impact on the management role. But the technology itself is universal; that is, it operates according to impersonal dynamics that are independent of any given culture, national or corporate. This technology is a force for management homogeneity.

There is another set of arguments in favour of management homogeneity that derive from the relations between countries, which also change over time. Starting at the beginning, it would be reasonable to say that management emerged as a subject in the last twenty years of the nineteenth century. The 1880s saw the foundation of the first business schools in the USA (and for that matter in France) and the beginning of a management literature. However the degree of contact between countries (or the rate of international encounter to use the trendy phrase) was low before the end of Second World War (1939–45). Until the second half of the twentieth century only the upper classes travelled, and they did so for amusement rather than for work, business or interorganisational coordination. As the twentieth century draws to a close only about 16 per cent of Americans have passports, so imagine what it was like in 1925!

Now in this situation where nobody travels much and no one knows very much about anywhere else, there is a dearth of evidence concerning possible country-based variations in a major occupational group such as management. Especially where there are universal forces for conformity of the kind we have already indicated, the natural tendency was to assume that everyone managed in pretty much the same way. This cosy state of insularity leading to assumptions of uniformity was shattered by the Second World War and developments after it.

It is commonly accepted that the Second World War produced two super-powers, the USA and the former USSR (communist Russia as it existed from 1917–91), but only one of these, the USA, was an economic superpower. It organised the world economic system to its satisfaction at the Bretton Woods conference in 1944 (Thurow, 1992), and it constituted the biggest and most affluent market for 30 years or more thereafter. Unit costs tended to be lower because of the need for large-volume production (the economy of scale argument) and there was a powerful incentive for new product development. The USA itself was the first and best market for new products and technical innovations. All this gave American companies an advantage overseas – they had the newest products at the lowest cost – and American manufacturing subsidiaries proliferated in postwar Europe.

Side by side with its economic supremacy the USA pioneered business education. The USA had more universities than any other country, a higher proportion of the relevant age group went to college, and most colleges offered business studies. By the 1950s the USA had more students of business administration than of any other subject (Whye, 1955), and American academics dominated the development of management as a subject. Marketing and corporate strategy are virtually American creations. Something like 85 per cent of all the books that have ever been written on management have been written by Americans. The USA also pioneered the MBA.

These two issues – American economic leadership and American virtuosity in management techniques and training – conjoined after the Second World War to produce the much vaunted 'management gap' (Locke, 1996). The management gap paralleled the technology gap. It denoted the extent to which management in other countries (Europe) fell behind that in the USA.

So the USA, its methods and standards, became a model for postwar reconstruction in Europe. The USA manfully shouldered the responsibility for Europe's managerial regeneration, and established the Joint Productivity Council (Locke, 1996), the essence of which was that tens of thousands of European managers were taken to the USA, shown American companies in operation and given a course in American methods and systems. Then they went back to Europe and did what they had been taught.

The overall effect of this managerial *pax Americana* was to give a boost to presumptions of managerial homogeneity, albeit in a rather different way. American leadership established a model and a single standard of managerial practice. Some companies – and indeed by aggregating companies, some countries – might have fallen short of the standard, were found to be wanting, but they all knew what they were 'shooting for'! American efficiency was universally recognised and praised. Those well-run American companies with their all-encompassing systems (Lawrence, 1996) seemed absolutely unstoppable to the Europeans. In France in particular American corporate penetration became a national *cause célèbre*, and a book documenting its threat to the economic integrity of France became a best seller (Servan-Schreiber, 1967). European managers lucky enough to be hired by American subsidiaries recognised the promised land when it was shown to them (they also received higher salaries). They were typically euphoric about American systems, American resources and the general 'can do' ethos that was the American corporate trademark in the postwar period. Such Europeans knew that their American experience would give them a corporate career edge, that they need never look back.

So just when the countries of the industrialised world were getting to know more about each other (and might have started to notice non-superficial differences) one of their number, the USA, moved into the driving seat by professing universal and therefore unifying standards. Insofar as there were any differences in management style and practice, it was felt that they would be progressively reduced as the companies of other countries adopted American best practice.

In the postwar period yet another force operated against the recognition of country-based differences, and this centred not on the relations between nations but upon nationalism. The essence of this is as follows. The Nazi regime in Germany (1933–45), the black scourge of Europe, was bound up with convictions, indeed declarations, of national greatness, national superiority and national destiny – and the price the world paid was the most widespread war in history and the death of an estimated 55 million, including about 6 million victims of the holocaust and 20 million citizens of the USSR. In the quarter century or so after the Second World War it was simply 'not on' to talk about national identity, national character or national difference. More soberly, to treat nationality, or the nation state, as a major differentiating or explanatory variable would have been ethically and philosophically suspect.

Indeed this un-nationally conscious period witnessed another force for homogenisation in the sense that the rapidly expanding discipline of sociology came up with the idea of convergence theory (Kerr *et al.*, 1960). The essence of convergence theory was that the industrialised and democratic states of the world were coming to resemble each other more and more, were marked by political moderation, growing affluence, consumerism and a pluralistic distribution of power between capital and labour. At its height, disciples of convergence theory sometimes went as far as to suggest that these developments, especially affluence and consumerism, would eventually modify the sharp division between capitalist and communist states.

We have rehearsed this battery of arguments in favour of presumptions of management homogeneity for two reasons. First, this view held sway for a long time. Second, for the most part the thesis is sensible. Companies do strive for profit, and cost reduction and efficiency are universal means to that end, the USA did provide a dominant model of management, working-class affluence in the postwar world has made for a modicum of cross-country similarity, and so on. What we have to recognise is that, despite these valid reasons for expecting homogeneity, there is evidence to suggest that a whole range of differences exist in business systems, management styles and corporate postures on a country-to-country basis.

Turning point

Nineteen seventy-seven saw the publication of Theodore Weinshall's book *Culture and Management*, an edited collection of writings illuminating the impact of culture on management style and values. The collection includes some contributions from Weinshall himself, and their provenance is quite fascinating.

Weinshall is an Israeli with an American doctorate. He undertook a series of visiting professorships at INSEAD, the international business school outside

Paris, and he used these visits to study the (interactive) behaviour of managers from different countries on post-experience courses by means of observation, tests, questionnaires, reports on their home companies and so on. One example, just to give the flavour of Weinshall's innovative work, concerns the propensity of managers from different countries to form relationships (talk to) managers from other countries on the same course. It should be noted that language ability was not a determinant of this behaviour since fluency in English and/or French was a prerequisite for attendance. It emerged that the Canadians communicated most with managers from other countries, followed by the Americans. The British were more reserved, but were surpassed in this by the French, who in the main spoke only to each other.

Weinshall also asked these managers to report on the level of verbal inter-action at their employing companies: to whom they spoke, and how often. Again sizeable differences emerged between the Anglo-Saxons (and the Israelis), who tended be frequent verbal communicators, that is, they fre-quently engaged in face-to-face communication or communiction by internal telephone, and the French managers, whose verbal communication tended to be rather sparse and limited to formal meetings. The French, on the other hand, made much more use of written communication.

Now there are probably a lot of people who would say that these findings could have been expected, that this is what they would have suggested if asked the leading question. Nonetheless it is to Weinshall's credit that he was the first to document some of these differences, even if they have now passed into 'common expectation' if not common knowledge.

Cross-cultural studies

Since Weinshall there have been several cross-cultural studies of managers or organisational employees that show a range of culture-based differences. The most famous of these is the work of the Dutch psychologist Geert Hofstede, whose survey data on IBM employees in the 40 countries in which IBM then operated is the basis of a brilliant interpretative study (Hofstede, 1980). As is well known, Hofstede perceived four key dimensions:

- Individualism versus collectivism.
- Power distance (willingness or otherwise to accept differences in power).
- Masculinity versus femininity (in the sense of output and achievement versus quality and relationship values).
- Uncertainty avoidance.

He then plotted the 40 countries in accordance with these four dimensions. What in simple terms emerged was a lot of variation in the way each of the countries was placed on these four dimensions, the demonstration of difference being all the more cogent when one remembers that the respondents were all employees of the same US multinational company. No only was there a broad contrast between developing countries and industrialised countries, with for instance the former tending to be collectivist and the latter individualist, but also differences between the industrialised countries themselves. Take for example the findings on uncertainty avoidance. Table 10.1 shows the finding for a few key countries in Hofstede's presentation.

Striking differences. This more or less says that the Germans are nearly twice as keen to avoid uncertainty as the British, and the French have even stronger uncertainty avoidance tendencies. It should be noted that for Britain, France and Germany these varying responses to the threat of uncertainty are broadly reflected in the national language. French lends itself to clarity and precision, the German language is admirably suited to serious and complicated exegeses, while English tends to be a little treasury of vagueness, understatement and gentle allusion.

There is also an organisational reflection of these responses to uncertainty, particularly in the French case. The classic depiction of French organisational life by Michel Crozier (1964) drew attention to its strongly bureaucratic nature. Now bureaucracy with its emphasis on rules, procedures, hierarchies, tight definitions of task and responsibility, and its penchant for conducting business in writing all serve to remove uncertainty. Crozier's characterisation was substantially confirmed by a later and more broadly based study (Barsoux and Lawrence, 1997), which draws attention to the elitist hierarchy and the impersonal nature of work relations in French companies. Michael

TABLE 10.1 Uncertainty avoidance

	Score
Greece	112
France	86
Austria	76
(West) Germany	65
USA	46
Britain	35
Singapore	8

A high score means a strong tendency to avoid uncertainty. Greece had the highest score of the 40 countries and Singapore had the lowest.
Source: Hofstede, 1980.

Johnson, an American who has held a senior management post in a French company, writes in his largely autobiographical account that French staff use the formalities of the organisation, particularly the written definitions of their duties, to limit their contribution (Johnson, 1997).

What a non-French person notices when walking about a French organisation is the absence of social closeness and overt chumminess. One looks in vain for the clubiness of many British work groups or the instant sociability of American ones. Still, whether or not one is attracted to the more controlled and impersonal work environment in France, it does reduce uncertainty – about performance, about requirements, about what the individual is charged to do.

Returning to Hofstede's study, the Germans exhibited stronger uncertainty-avoidance drives than the British, and this was also identifiable in German companies. Indeed the present author spent a lot of time as an observer in German manufacturing companies and was struck by their operational efficiency. Nothing ever seemed to go wrong: there were no breakdowns, no power cuts, they never ran out of anything, there were no labour problems, no shortages, and everything got done on time. All this did not happen of its own accord, it happened because energy, intention and resources went into making it happen. The structure and ethos of German companies seems oriented towards avoiding nasty surprises! In other words, if uncertainty is seen as threatening, the threat may be reduced by meticulous planning and organisation.

There is another characteristically German response to the threat of uncertainty: reliance on experts. Expert input is an antidote to uncertainty because the expert will be able to define situations authoritatively and say what has to be done. This attachment to expertise is very clear in German management, which has a strongly specialist rather than generalist orientation (Lawrence, 1980). That is, unlike the British the Germans do not put their faith in social and political skills conjoined with an overall view, and unlike the Americans they do not emphasise energy, adaptability, and a mastery of relevant management systems. German companies, when recruiting, assigning and advancing professional and managerial staff, emphasise specialist knowledge and relevant experience. That is, they value knowledge and experience that are relevant to particular jobs, functions and industries. With regard to first-job applicants they are more interested in the content of the courses taken than with titular qualifications or the prestige of the institution that awarded it. Thereafter recruits advance primarily in the function they have joined – design, production, engineering, personnel, finance or whatever – and are unlikely to change industry, though judicious moves between different companies in the same industry are acceptable.

Hofstede (1980) tells an instructive story on this theme of the German attachment to the specialist by comparing medical expenditure in his native Holland with that of Germany. Investigating, what proportion of the total was spent on doctors and on nurses in each country, he found that Holland spent more on nurses and Germany spent more on doctors. And what was Germany getting for its money by favouring doctors? It was getting experts who would tell them what it was all about, and remove uncertainty.

Hofstede's IBM data is from the 1970s, with the key work 'Culture's Consequences' published in 1980. A French management teacher, André Laurent, collected cross-cultural data in the 1980s. Like Weinshall (1977), Laurent (1990) conducted his research at INSEAD, asking managers from different countries to respond to a battery of propositions about management work and its context. We shall look at one or two examples adapted from a presentation made by Laurent at the Strategic Management Society's annual conference at Stockholm in 1990. The first concerns the role of conflict in organisations (Table 10.2).

There are two points of interest here. The first is the range of difference. The respondents were all managers, no doubt working for leading companies in their countries, well thought of by their companies, or enough to be sent on expensive training courses at INSEAD. The only way in which they differed was by nationality, but the impact of nationality seems to be such that, in this case, the Italians were *ten times* more concerned to eliminate conflict from organisational life than were the Swedes.

The second point of interest is that where national groups expressed similar views, or responded to a proposition in approximately the same way, it may have been for different reasons – though this is my interpretation rather than that of André Laurent. Take for example the Swedes' and the Americans' response to the proposition about conflict, and ask why the Swedes seemed to have little concern about suppressing conflict. It one puts this question to students the usual response is to say that Sweden as a society does not have much conflict, so its elimination is not an issue. This is indeed the image that

TABLE 10.2 Managerial responses to the statement 'It would be good if conflict in organisations could be eliminated for ever'

	Percentage of managers who agree
Sweden	4
USA	6
Britain	13
Germany	16
France	24
Italy	41

Source: Laurent, 1990.

Sweden enjoys in the wider world (in Bill Bryson's lighthearted travel book *Neither Here Nor There* there is a joke that the way to start a revolution in Sweden is to take your library books back late).

But there are other considerations in the case of Sweden, of which the most general is the fact that patience, restraint and reasonableness are public virtues in Swedish society. This makes conflict, whether there is a lot or a little of it, rather less of a threat because disagreements, opposed opinions or conflicting 'war aims' can usually be resolved in a non-violent and relatively non-disruptive way (Lawrence and Spybey, 1986). What is more Swedish industry has an elaborate codetermination system, constructed piecemeal in the 1960s and 1970s. Unlike the German system, the Swedish one does not confer specific rights on workers and workers' representatives but gives them the right to negotiate with management. This is very instructive. The implication is that negotiation rights are valuable in that they lead to a reasonable, probably compromise-based resolution of contested issues. *Ipso facto* conflict is not a worry.

But what of the Americans? Are they also indifferent to the repression of conflict because they are inherently reasonable and love compromise? The present writer once showed a transparency of Laurent's findings on conflict to a group of managers drawn from several countries, and invited their comments on the small proportion of Americans concerned to suppress conflict. An American in the front row volunteered the thought: 'We are not bothered about conflict because we expect to win.' A second American added to this testimony: 'And we carry guns!' There was no doubt a jocular side to these responses, but they certainly expressed a rather un-Swedish disposition. In a society that is strongly individualist (it came top on individualism in Hofstede's 40 countries) and strongly committed to achievement, conflict is inevitable, but it is seen as a test of manhood rather than a social evil. After all, as the logo on a popular American T-shirt expresses it: 'Failure is not an option'.

A similar pattern of response arises in another of Laurent's propositions, this time concerning hierarchy (Table 10.3).

The same divergence of opinion occurs here. Four fifths of the Swedes thought it was alright to by-pass the hierarchy, but three quarters of the Italians were opposed. The Italians' response was consistent with their response regarding conflict, that is if you are worried about conflict in organisations to the point of wanting to suppress it altogether, you are likely to support the hierarchy as the instrument of order and control. On the other hand the Swedes, with their pronounced egalitarian values, were uncomfortable with the very idea of hierarchy, which makes nasty distinctions between people. As every Swede knows: 'En man är lika god som en an' (every man/person is as good as everyone else).

The American response, where two-thirds of those questioned were quite happy to by-pass the hierarchy, is not quite so easy to interpret. But a probable

TABLE 10.3   **Managerial responses to the proposition 'To get things done you sometimes have to by-pass the hierarchy'**

	Percentage of managers who disagree
Sweden	22
USA	32
Britain	31
France	42
Germany	46
Italy	75

Source: Laurent, 1990.

TABLE 10.4   **Managerial responses to the proposition 'A manager must have precise answers for questions subordinates raise about work'**

	Percentage of managers who agree
Sweden	10
USA	18
Britain	27
Germany	46
France	53
Italy	66

Source: Laurent, 1990.

explanation is that most of the Americans acknowledged to themselves that they would by-pass the hierarchy if they felt they had to or that it would be to their advantage. Then of course they would hope to be proved right, that they would be forgiven for the organisational infraction and their standing would be enhanced.

Another of Laurent's propositions is about whether managers should be able to answer subordinates' questions (Table 10.4), and again it has implications for order, hierarchy and the legitimisation of authority.

Again the same extraordinary spread, with the Italians nearly seven times more concerned to answer subordinates' questions authoritatively than the Swedes. So what is going on here? A speculative interpretation would be that:

- The Swedes did not like the sound of having to answer subordinates' questions, it smacked of hierarchy and dominance and offended their egalitarianism.
- The Americans thought it a bit naïve; management is about power and achievement not messing around giving people precise answers.
- The British thought 'precise answers' sounded a bit boring, something the 'higher-ups' could leave to the 'lower-downs', who lack generalist vision.
- The Germans saw a tacit appeal to expert power and specialist knowledge and nearly half of them responded positively.
- The French managers were conscious of their educational and intellectual superiority, and it followed that precise answers were in order. The majority concurred.
- The Italians, troubled as ever by intimations of organisational chaos and the breakdown of order, would welcome the opportunity for the manager to reinforce the hierarchy with a display of superior knowledge.

There is another thread running through these responses, and this concerns the managers' understanding of the management role. Is management work about knowing, or about doing? It is probable that none of the national groups would give a clear-cut answer to this question, but it is also likely that there would be a graduation of emphasis, with the Italians and to a lesser extent the French seeing management as legitimised by its knowledge, managers being professionals drawing on 'management science' as doctors draw on medical science.

Management contrasts at the end of the century

In addition to the Weinshall, Hofstede and Laurent studies from the 1970s and 1980s, there is survey data collected by the present author and Barbara Senior in the late 1990s. Our study was along the same lines as that of André Laurent in that groups of practising managers, mainly from European countries, were confronted with propositions about business and management, to which they responded on a five-point scale ranging from strongly agree to strongly disagree. The sample was accessed primarily via post-experience courses at Nene College and via that college's partner institutions in other countries; we will call it the Nene study and will 'dip into it' here to confirm earlier findings and extend the appreciation of management difference.

Managers from Italy had a distinctive profile in the Laurent study, so for a start we put the Italian scores beside those for a larger group of British managers. This exercise yielded two kinds of differences. There were some items where the mean score for one country put the Italians on the 'agree' side of the scale while the mean score for the other group put them on the 'disagree' side, and there were far more instances where the differences between the two groups were statistically significant, where both groups agreed or disagreed but with different degrees of emphasis. We will draw on the first set, the agree versus disagree cases, to highlight some features of Italian management and to point up the contrast with British management.

The first thing to emerge was the fact that some of the Italians seemed to have a rather old-fashioned, formalistic view of management, which was also evident in the Laurent study. For instance the proposition 'Organisational success comes from maintaining a stable organisation structure where everyone knows their role and position and works within it' was accepted by the Italians but rejected by the British. This suggests a rather Henri Fayol-type classical management view on the part of the Italian managers. Consistent with this they tended towards a rather directive view of the manager's role, for example the proposition 'Most employees like to be told what to do' was accepted by the Italians but rejected by the British. Likewise the proposition 'Employees at all levels should be consulted on matters of company policy and operation' was accepted by the British but rejected by the Italians, whose implicit view seemed to be that managers are there to tell people what to do, not to consult subordinates.

This view emerged again in response to a proposition about worker representation on the board of directors: 'Employees should be represented on the boards of companies to protect worker's interests when policy decisions are made'. This was accepted by the British but rejected by the Italians. Ironically Britain has no industrial democracy legislation on the statute book and is often berated for this by its more enlightened EU partners; Italy does have some industrial democracy provision written into its postwar constitution but it is questionable whether this amounts to much in practice.

The concern to avert conflict, evident in the Laurent findings, was replicated in the Nene study. The proposition 'Conflict is necessary in organisations as an antidote to complacency' was accepted by the British but rejected by the Italians. Likewise the proposition 'Conflict over scarce resources is inevitable in most organisations' was accepted by the British but rejected by the Italians, as was the proposition 'Employees should be able to challenge the views and decisions of management'. But the Italians did accept the proposition 'At the end of the day, most managers want subordinates who are loyal rather than critical and challenging', although the British rejected it. This preference for loyalty over other qualities is something the Italians seem to share with managers from Arab countries, according to Farid Muna's twelve-country study (Muna, 1980). Another proposition that differentiated the Italians from the British was 'Managers, because of their status, are entitled to respect from their subordinates', which the Italians accepted and the British rejected; perhaps the British are not as deferential as one supposes.

In short the juxtaposition of British and Italian responses from the Nene study does show a pattern of difference, and with regard to the Italians there is a high degree of consistency with some of André Laurent's findings.

Before moving on there are two other items that are revealing with regard to both countries. The proposition 'Management work today is all about meeting specific and short term targets' was accepted by the British and rejected by the Italians. The British were no doubt rightly acknowledging the short-termism endemic in the business world. This was probably less salient for the Italians, but one wonders if there was also an element of *bella figura* here because of the Italians' desire to put on a good face. If this was the case then the Italian managers might have rejected this proposition on the ground that it was somewhat demeaning to depict oneself as merely an instrument to realise short-term goals, probably set by someone else!

The other interesting proposition, that 'The engineering function should be an obvious path to senior positions in manufacturing industry', was rejected by the British and accepted by the Italians. The fact that engineers enjoy lower status in Britain than in the continental European countries is well documented and generally acknowledged (Hutton and Lawrence, 1981). Acceptance of this proposition on the Italian side no doubt signified the higher standing of professional engineers in that country. There is also a suggestion here of an Italian desire to see management in general as professional and knowledge-based, with academic credentials reinforcing hierarchical position. It is of a piece with the Italian response to Laurent's proposition about managers giving precise answers to their subordinates' questions.

The Second World War is over

Over half a century after the fall of the Third Reich and the end of the Second World War there is a residual view that Germans tend towards authoritarian submission, towards *a Befehl ist Befehl* (orders are orders) mentality. In the light of such a presumption it is intriguing to put the results of the Nene study for the Germans and the British side by side. This juxtaposition does not lend any credence to the view of Germans as submissive to authority, indeed the Germans emerge from the comparison as more critical, more challenging and less deferential than the British.

In response to the proposition 'Everyone, whatever their status, should have the right to say what they think' the Germans agreed more strongly than the British. This was also the case with the proposition 'Employees at all levels should be consulted on matters of company policy and operation'. This proposition had divided the British and the Italians on an agree versus disagree basis, but the Germans agreed with this proposition even more strongly than the British. Similarly the Germans took a more positive view of conflict than the British. The proposition 'Conflict is necessary in organisations as an antidote to complacency' was accepted more strongly by the Germans than the British, and the consistency-checking proposition 'Conflict is best regarded as evidence that senior management don't know how to manage' was rejected more strongly by the Germans than the British. In this connection it is also worth mentioning that in Hofstede's study (1980) the Germans and the British both ranked fairly low on the power distance scale, that is to say, in both cases there was little readiness to accept big differences in organisational power. In fact Hofstede ranked Britain and Germany exactly the same on the power distance scale.

The view that Germans have a mild tendency to engage in bureaucracy finds some support in the Nene study. The proposition 'Organisational success comes from maintaining a stable organisational structure where everyone knows their role and position and works within it' was accepted by the Germans, as it was by the Italians, though the British rejected it. This proposition no doubt appeals to German tidy-mindedness, to an *Ordnung muss sein* (there must be order) proclivity. On the other hand the proposition 'It is good practice to confirm in writing any agreements or decisions made during conversation' was rejected by the Germans while the British accepted it. On the British side this may represent not so much a desire for bureaucratic closure as a pervasive fear of being 'stitched up'!

When one put the German and British responses side by side there were several instances to suggest that the British felt more oppressed. For instance the proposition 'Greater pressure, in the sense of more targets and controls, is a key change in the manager's job in recent years' was affirmed more strongly by the British than by the Germans. Likewise the proposition 'Downsizing, delayering and collapsing of organisational boundaries adds to the work load of those who remain', and the proposition 'The systematic measurement of managers' performance detracts from motivation and commitment to the organisation' both received a more heartfelt response from the British than from the Germans.

Another theme that was highlighted by the Anglo-German comparison is the *Technik* orientation of German managers, their belief that if a company has good products everything else will follow. The proposition 'Today well-made products for which there is a known demand are likely to ensure a company's profitability' was accepted by both groups of managers, but more strongly by the Germans. This was also true of the proposition: 'Organisations with quality products and a motivated workforce will prosper whichever political party is in office'. These are both propositions that no one is likely to deny as it would be like burning the flag, but the degrees of affirmation are clearly significant.

The German responses also served to remind us that Germany is actually the world's largest exporter. The proposition 'It is increasingly important for companies to take account of the actions of competitors in other countries, and to preempt or respond to these actions in order to stay ahead' was affirmed more enthusiastically by the Germans than by the British, as was the proposition 'In my industry internationalisation is a key development in the 1990s'.

Finally, the proposition that divided the British and the Italians, that 'Management work today is all about meeting specific and short-term targets', was also denied by the Germans, though not by a large margin.

Systematising difference

At the start of this chapter we suggested that there were three answers to the question 'would you expect management to be the same in different countries?' The first answer was yes – we gave reasons for this view and noted that it has persisted for 80 years or more. The second view was no, and we reviewed evidence from cross-cultural studies from the 1970s to the late 1990s. The third view is yes there are differences, but it is still possible to pattern and group them, one does not have to treat every country as unique. It is to this third view that we now turn.

To begin with it should be said that the second view (there are differences) and the third view (we can plot and pattern them) are not distinct in a true sense. The two have overlapped and intermingled in the 1980s and 1990s, and in some cases they have interpenetrated. Hofstede's 1980 study for example, is the most famous demonstration of country-based differences in work-related values and at the same time an imaginative exercise in creating dimensions into which survey data can be assimilated.

The next thing to say is that the patterning has occurred in two different ways. The first has been to group sets of countries, usually contiguous ones, and to say that they are similar. Examples would be Arab countries, Anglo-Saxon countries or Scandinavian countries. The second approach has been analytical rather than ostensive, and has consisted of proposing some analytical dimensions in terms of which countries can be plotted to yield groups or sets of countries in the same quadrant.

Let us begin with the analysers and proposers of classifying criteria. A writer whose work has attracted a lot of interest and attention in the 1990s is the Dutch management trainer and consultant Fons Trompenaars. In his principal work (Trompenaars, 1993) he has borrowed ideas from theoretical sociology, specifically what are known to sociologists as 'pattern variables', which were developed by the American sociologist Talcott Parsons in the 1950s (Parsons, 1951). These pattern variables are five pairs of counterpoised opposites that may be used to classify societies. They are:

- Universalism versus particularism.
- Collectivism versus individualism.
- Affectivity versus emotional neutrality.
- Specific versus diffuse.
- Achievement versus ascription.

Their function in the hands of Parsons and his school was to define social relationships, which would in turn characterise a society as modern or traditional. So modern or industrial society is held to be typified by relationships that are individual, specific and emotionally neutral, judged by criteria that are universal, with status being achieved rather than ascribed (inherited). More traditional societies are the reverse – collective, particular, affective and diffuse, with roles and status being ascribed. What Fons Trompenaars has done is to take these broad distinctions from sociology and rerun them to classify country-based business cultures, with some grouping around the axes.

This complex of classificatory ideas is refined in another book, written jointly by Trompenaars and the British academic Charles Hampden-Turner (Hampden-Turner and Trompenaars, 1993). In this version the authors use some of Parsons' pattern variables together with some new linked pairs:

- Analysing versus integrating.
- Inner directed (driven by own conscience and resolution) versus outer-directed (responding to outside cues).
- Time as sequence versus time as syncronisation.
- Equality versus hierarchy.

The set of variables is then used to classify types of capitalism, the ensuing book being entitled *The Seven Cultures of Capitalism*.

Trompenaars and Hampden-Turner are a little unusual in working with such a range of variables; more usual is classification according to two or three variables. A good example here is the work of the retired British banker John Mole. In a book engagingly entitled *Mind Your Manners* (1990), Mole suggested that organisations could be classified in terms of two dimensions: the prevalence of group leadership versus the prevalence of individual leadership; and whether they are systematic, with rational order imposed, or organic, where the organisation reflects and adapts to the needs and relationships of the members. The two axes are then crossed to yield quadrants in which countries can be located.

Another two-dimensional system is that of the well-known American couple Edward and Mildred Hall (Hall and Hall, 1990). First they counterpoise a monochronic and a polychronic understanding of time. Monochronic time, the Western model, treats time as a sequence; you start something, work on it, complete it, and then do something else. It is undesirable to interrupt the sequence (bad time management) and one should respect the integrity of other people's time sequences. On the other hand the polychronic orientation treats time as flux: it is fine to do several things at once, with different start and stop points, it is OK to interrupt the sequence and refocus later, this is how you show your verve.

The other variable used by the Halls is the idea of high-context versus low-context societies. A high-context society is one where most of the meaning is supplied by the relationships, the situations and the norms and values that underpin the society, while explicit communications, words actively spoken, convey only a small part of the meaning, perhaps are merely symbolic. Traditional societies are usually held to be high context, and Japan is usually seen as the example *par excellance* of the high-context society, where yes may mean yes or no – you have to work it out for yourself but if you were Japanese you would understand. On the other hand the West is generally held to be low context. That is, a particular situation tells you relatively little, but overt communication, the words themselves, convey the message. America, with its penchant for declaratory frankness, is a splendid example of the low context in action. If the Japan versus USA contrast is felt to be too obvious, then one could run this high context versus low context distinction in Europe, or at least in terms of relative emphasis. So for example Italy, with its greater emphasis on relationship and interactional subtext would be higher context than Sweden; Austria would be higher context than Germany.

A variation on this theme of dimensional classification is to take countries or groups of countries as models, as representing a particular value or activating principle. One writer to have done this is the Spanish diplomat Salvador de Madariaga (1992, 1996). The essence of his thesis is that Europe has three paratypical countries:

- France: the country of thought and administrative right.
- England: the country of action and fair play.
- Spain: the country of honour and passion.

These three are both paratypical and models to which other cultures may aspire or approximate. A more recent (British) variation on this theme is the work of Gatley and Lessem (1995), who classify regions in terms of a dominant orientation:

- Western: action oriented.
- Northern: thought oriented.
- Southern: family oriented.
- Eastern: group oriented.

While these may be rather loose attributions they accommodate much of our experience and perception of other countries.

The idea of grouping contiguous countries, those that form a 'national' or regional bloc, is popular with people writing about other countries on the basis of their own work experience as managers, consultants or journalists. An example from the 1990s is Richard Hill's *We Europeans* (1992). This is a witty, entertaining, insightful and experience-based account, and it is noticeable that the author uses the grouping technique. For example Norway, Sweden, Finland and Denmark are lumped together, as are the 'Slav countries', although Hill notes *en passant* that Hungary and Estonia do not actually speak a Slavonik language.

But the most frequently quoted paper favouring the (usually) contiguous group of countries approach is that of Ronen and Shenkar (1985). Their groupings are shown in Figure 10.1. What gives particular weight to the Ronen and Shenkar configuration is that they have constructed it on the basis of eight questionnaire studies of job orientation and values conducted by other researchers.

Source: Ronen and Shenkar, 1985.

FIGURE 10.1   Countries grouped by management culture

The account in this section of the work of those who have sought to systematise the similarities and differences between countries is illustrative rather than exhaustive, but it is hoped that the main lines of the systematising operation have been made clear. But is the systematising effort helpful, desirable or worthwhile?

Progress at a price

It has to be admitted that systematising endeavours do involve some risk of simplification, misapprehension or even distortion. A very basic consideration is that if one elects to classify phenomena – say business cultures – in terms of one or two dimensions, then however relevant and insightful these dimensions are, they are only part of the picture, and the rest is discarded. In an extreme case the effect can be disturbing, separating entities that common sense tells us belong together, or putting in the same box things that are manifestly different. Supposing one wants a schema for classifying well-known people. One might have good reason to decide that a key variable is whether or not the books a person had written were banned during his or her lifetime. And one might decide that another psychologically revealing variable is whether or not someone had a pet dog. One could construct a two by two table with just these two variables, in which case Enid Blyton and Adolf Hitler would both fit into the top-left-hand box of Figure 10.2.

Of course this is a contrived and absurd example, but it demonstrates the logical possibilities. John Mole, using his individual versus collective leader-

	Books banned	Books not banned
Pet dog		
No pet dog		

FIGURE 10.2

ship and his systematic versus organic organisations, puts Germany and the USA in the same quadrant. It is not a mistake, they are both individual and systematic; but is it illuminating when one considers the manifold and manifest differences in business culture and management style between Germany and the USA?

A second issue in these attempts at classificatory systematisation is that the dimensions used may be differently understood. Consider for example Hofstede's individualism versus collectivism dimension. Two countries are in joint thirteenth place in the individualism table: France and Sweden. Now Hofstede no doubt used measures that resulted in France and Sweden receiving equal scores. The popular view, however, would be that France is a highly individualist country whereas the welfare and egalitarian values in Sweden engender a mild conformism. And on this occasion the popular view is telling us something. It is drawing attention to the fact that France is high on what one might call expressive individualism – style, wit, élan, cleverness, intellectual creativity, personal wilfulness and so on. Yet Hofstede's study is clearly measuring something different: the USA comes out on top for individualism, followed by a group of Anglo-Saxon countries. Clearly what is being measured is economic individualism and achievement drives. Perfectly reasonable of course, but it does not have to be this way. It could have been expressive individualism. What about Gerard de Nerval taking his pet lobster for walks in the streets of Paris?

A third problem with these classifying dimensions is that the entities one wants to classify do not come ready labelled. There is not, as it were, a sign at Heathrow saying 'Welcome to the UK. This is a low context society. We have a sequential concept of time'. The dimensions are typically analytical and abstract; consider for example those deployed by Fons Trompenaars and Charles Hampden-Turner. And because the dimensions are abstract and the entities to be classified are unlabelled, one needs to find, perhaps designate is a better word, some indicators. And this operation is neither artless nor faultless.

We might again take the Hofstede study as offering a good example of the extend to which indicators may backfire. Denmark is a country that 'does well' on Hofstede's uncertainty avoidance dimension. That is, the Danes exhibit low uncertainty avoidance, or to put it more positively, show a high tolerance for change and/or ambiguity. However if one examines Hofstede's small print it emerges that much of this low uncertainty avoidance rating arose because of the way the Danes responded to questions such as 'Do you intend to change your job in the next two years or so?' A large proportion of the Danes said yes to this, and Hofstede quite reasonably took it to indicate a positive attitude towards change. Fine, so far. But why are these Danes going to change jobs? Well apart from the Carlsberg brewery, celebrated in Chapter 3, and the A.P. Møllers shipping company, Denmark has no big companies, so managers and professionals advance their careers by making diagonal moves between companies (I am indebted to my friend Jette Schramm of the Copenhagen Business School for this insight). So even if the Danes do have a high tolerance for ambiguity, job changing does not provide evidence of this.

We might also spare a thought for the systematising endeavour that groups countries by origin or contiguity. This endeavour reaches a high point of scholarly substance in the Ronen and Shenkar typology reproduced in Figure 10.1. Most readers will probably feel they are most familiar with the Anglo-Saxon countries on Ronen and Shenker's list, that is, Britain, the USA, Canada, Australia and New Zealand. Now there is clearly some justification for this grouping. These countries have a common language, a common heritage, are predominantly Christian Protestant, are all parliamentary democracies, are all linked to Britain in terms of a colonial past, were all on the same side in the two world wars, and so on. But this does not make them identical. If we take the lead countries, Britain and the USA, one might note that:

- Americans believe everything is possible; the British believe nothing changes.
- Americans believe in programmed leadership; the British believe in charismatic leadership.
- Americans put their trust in management systems; the British believe in management discretion.
- Americans overcommunicate; Britons undercommunicate.
- Americans have kept labour unions at bay; Britain has a strong trade union tradition.
- Americans practice 'hire and fire'; the British like the idea of it.
- Americans think big is beautiful, and like to do things on large scale; the British think big is vulgar, and like to rely on ingenuity and resourcefulness.
- American managers are like each other: 'a flock of aggressive sheep' as the Canadians say; British managers are often idiosyncratic; there is plenty of role variance.
- American managers use power openly to get things done and 'remove road blocks'; the British use power hesitantly and indirectly; they rule by innuendo.
- The American manager would most like to be a business owner; the British manager would most like to go to a garden party at Buckingham Palace.

Now suppose you know as much about South America or about East Central Europe as you do about Britain and the USA, is it not possible that you would see differences of comparable magnitude between Latvia and Ukraine, or between Argentina and Peru? And do you have any thoughts about Israel being in the same box as Germany, Sweden and Switzerland?

Understanding in one country

We have raised some concerns about attempts to systematise differences between countries and their business cultures and management values. Clearly there are gains from these schemas, gains of insight, of the benefit of putting disparate entities at different points on the same dimension, gains of intellectual economy. At the same time there is a downside: the risk of misapprehension and oversimplification.

Before ending this chapter we would like to put the case for treating the single country/nation state as the *point de dé part*, as the unit of analysis. In discussions about countries and the differences between them, culture is in the foreground. That is, the emphasis tends to be on the intangible on values and norms, orientations and thoughtways, nuances of behaviour and understanding. This is totally justified. These intangibles do matter, they are powerful forces in shaping behaviour and outcome, and it is intriguing to decode them and fun to talk about them. At the same time there is another perhaps more tangible level of reality. Consider that various countries all have:

- legislative capability – each has its own laws, and, for example, those of Argentina may not resemble those of Paraguay, even if they are both Spanish speaking, Catholic and next door;
- their own institutions, but these are valid only in the state concerned: institutions of education, vocational training, industrial relations and wage bargaining, worker democracy (or not), and so on;
- a variable past that will in some sense shape the present.

Laws and institutions are quite tangible; furthermore they stand behind national culture, values and consciousness and deserve our attention. Let us consider a specific example.

LEST (Laboratoire d'Economic et de Sociologie du Travail) is a research institute in Aix-en-Provence, France. In the 1970s LEST conducted two overlapping studies of companies in France and what was then West Germany. These were studies of matched companies, matched in the sense of being paired by product and by appropriate size, for example a French company making steel tubes and a German company making steel tubes, a French company making cardboard packaging and a German company making cardboard packaging, and so on.

The first LEST study, the one we shall discuss for illustrative purposes, was about salary hierarchies. A salary hierarchy is the gap between the highest paid person in an organisation and the lowest paid. The outcome of the salary hierarchy comparison is shown in Figure 10.3.

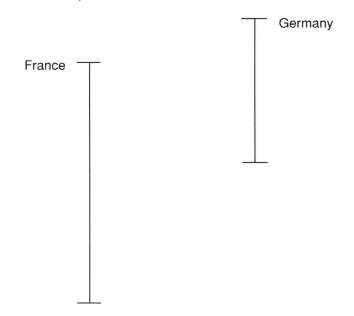

FIGURE 10.3   Salary hierarchies, France and Germany

The top point on the German scale is a little higher than that for France, and the mid point is higher than for France. This is not suprising, after all Germany is a richer country than France. What is significant is the fact that the French salary hierarchy scale is longer, that is, the gap between the highest paid person and the lowest paid person in the small group of French companies in the sample was larger than the corresponding gap in the German companies.

So far we have depicted the contrasting salary hierarchies in overall terms, but it is also possible to speak in specifics. In the French case:

- The gap between the chief executive and the next level down is larger than in Germany.
- The gap between higher management and middle management is larger than in Germany.
- The gap between middle mangers and white-collar workers is larger than in Germany.
- The gap between supervisors (foremen) and blue-collar workers is larger than in Germany.
- The gap between skilled, semi-skilled and unskilled workers is larger than in Germany.

How are we to explain the longer salary hierarchy in France? At the bottom of the French hierarchy there is a relatively weak apprenticeship system, and there is no particular valorisation of craft skill. Consequently there is a skills shortage and companies that have skilled workers need to pay them relatively more to keep them, to reward those scarce skills. So the differentials between unskilled, semiskilled, skilled and supervisors are larger than in Germany. At the top of the French hierarchy there is a greater spread of qualifications, whose differential reward is reflected in the extended French salary scale. In Germany, either one has been to university or one has not. In France it is not so simple. After taking and passing the baccalaureat (which in France is the equivalent of British A levels) the majority go to university. But this is not the only possibility. Some embark on the struggle to be admitted to a *grande école*. The first step in enrolment is an *école préparataire*, where one works extremely hard for some two years and then takes a nationally competitive examination, the *concours* for admission to the *grandes écoles* (Barsoux and Lawrence, 1997).

What precisely are these *grandes écoles*? They constitute the upper level of a two-tier system of higher education. There are about 140 to 160 of them, depending on whose figures you believe. They are relatively small, they recruit in terms of hundreds, whereas the universities recruit by tens of thousands, having to take (in the first instance) everyone qualified to enrol (those who have passed the baccalaureat). But among these exalted *grandes écoles* there are also graduations of status. Some are exceptionally prestigious (and difficult to get into), for example the *école polytechnique*. Others are fairly close in status to the *polytechnique*, but are considered as not quite as good. Hence there are *grandes écoles* and there are *petites écoles* or *écoles moins grandes*, but of course all of them are better than mere universities.

So both at the bottom there are craft and vocational qualifications, and at the top there is a two-tier system of higher education, where the top tier itself contains many graduations of status, and thus the spread of qualifications and credentials in France is very wide. This is reflected in the salary hierarchy, and that is why it is long by German standards.

But what of Germany. Is it simply a matter of 'educational compression' compared with France? Well the educational compression argument is certainly important. In Germany there are something like 460 occupations for which apprenticeships are available. Unlike in some countries, and Britain provides a contrast here, apprenticeship in Germany is not restricted to old-fashioned 'metal bashing' industries such as boilermaking and shipbuilding. In Germany the apprenticeship system seems to have developed to embrace 'second industrial revolution' industries: twentieth-century technologies and service industry occupations. Something like 65 per cent of the age group do an apprenticeship. When one also takes out the proportion of that age group that go to university, and the larger proportion that go to *Fachhochschulen* (an intermediate level offering three-year courses on a wide range of vocational subjects, especially technical ones – Hutton and Lawrence, 1981), there is not much left, not much of an 'educational tail' to extend the salary hierarchy downwards.

But there is more. Germany has a stronger trade union movement than France, where trade union power is somewhat diluted by the movement being split into several confederations along political and confessional lines. Not so in Germany, which has a system of 18 industrial unions that are strongly coordinated by a central umbrella organisation, the DGB (the German equivalent of the British TUC, but stronger and better resourced). Any German wishing to be a union member will join an industrial trade union, as opposed to a general or craft union, irrespective of their specific job and skill level. This makes these unions more focused, more unitary, and it also precludes the possibility of demarcation disputes (for which there is no set expression in German).

Pay bargaining in Germany is institutionalised and orderly. The deals are struck by negotiations between the BDA (the German employers' federation) and the relevant trade union at fixed and scheduled intervals on a *Land* by *Land* basis. (*Länder*, the plural of *Land*, are the various states that make up the Federal Republic of Germany, for example Bavaria. There are now 16 *Länder* as a result of the five East German ones joining the Western ones upon German reunification in 1990.) All this makes the wage system and wage rises stable and predictable most of the time (Lawrence, 1982). The trade union system has also been a force for raising blue-collar wages throughout most of the postwar period, which again has served to shorten the German salary hierarchy.

What is more Germany has a long-established system of codetermination of industrial democracy. In particular the system of elected works councils, established in 1951, is so much a part of the German industrial scene as to be described as an *Ordnungsfaktor* (a force for order). This industrial democracy system is a force for equality, for the safeguarding of employees' interests and for limiting the managerial prerogative. As we have seen in Chapter 6, this makes it more difficult for managers in German companies to act imperiously or on the spur of the moment: there can be no big discretionary rises, nor battlefield promotion. Changes in job category and wage group have to be confirmed by the works council.

What we have done in the last few pages is to take a significant fact of industrial culture – divergent salary hierarchies in matched industries in two countries – and explained the difference primarily in terms of institutions. That is, the variance has been explained with reference to the education and vocational training systems in France and Germany, the trade union wage bargaining system, and the effects of industrial democracy and codetermination legislation. In the eyes of Ronen and Shenkar (1985), Germany may be like Sweden and Switzerland in a broad cultural sense, but all these are sovereign states that may, and in fact do, differ in regard to the institutional variable explored in this discussion of the LEST studies.

In the next and final chapter we will raise a corresponding questions: is there any sense in which it is meaningful to speak of a European style of management?

References

Barsoux, J.-L. and P. A. Lawrence (1997) *French Management: Elitism in Action*, London: Cassell.

Crozier, Michel (1964) *The Bureaucratic Phenomenon*, London: Tavistock.

Gatley, S. and R. Lessem (1995) 'Enhancing the Competitive Advantage of Transcultural Businesses', *European Journal of Industrial Training*, vol. 19.

Hall, Edward T. and Mildred Reed Hall (1990) *Understanding Cultural Differences*, Yarnmouth, Maine: International Press.

Hill, Richard (1992) *We Europeans*, Brussels: Europublications.

Hampden-Turner, Charles and Fons Trompenaars (1993) *The Seven Cultures of Capitalism*, New York: Doubleday.

Hofstede, Geert (1980) *Culture's Consequences*, Beverly Hills, LA: Sage.

Hutton, S. P. and P. A. Lawrence (1981) *German Engineers: The Anatomy of a Profession*, Oxford: Clarendon Press.

Johnson, Michael (1997) *French Resistance*, London: Cassell.

Kerr, Clark, Dunlop, John T., Harbison, Frederick H., Myers, Charles (1960) *Industrialism and Industrial Man*, London: Heinemann.

Lawrence, Peter (1980) *Managers and Management in West Germany*, London: Croom Helm.

Lawrence, P. A. (1982) *Personnel Management in West Germany: Portrait of a Function*, Berlin: International Institute of Management and Administration.

Lawrence, Peter (1996) *Management in the USA*, London: Sage.

Lawrence, Peter and Tony Spybey (1986) *Management and Society in Sweden*, London: Routledge and Kegan Paul.

Locke, Robert (1996) *The Collapse of the American Management Mystique*, Oxford: Oxford University Press.

Madariaga, Salvador de (1922) *Englishman, Frenchman, Spaniard*, Oxford: Oxford University Press.

Madariaga, Salvador de (1966) *The Spirit of Europe*, London: Hollis and Carter.

Mole, John (1990) *Mind Your Manners*, London: The Industrial Society.

Muna, Farid (1980) *Arab Management*, New York: St Martin's Press.

Parsons, Talcott (1951) *The Social System*, Glencoe, Ill.: The Free Press.

Ronen, Simcha and Oded Shenkar (1985) 'Clustering Countries on Attitude and Dimensions: A Review and Synthesis', *Academy of Management Review*, vol. 10, no. 3, pp. 435–54.

Servan-Schreiber, J.-J. (1967) *Le défi Américain*, Paris: Denoel.

Thurow, Lester (1992) *Head to Head*, New York: William Morrow.

Trompenaars, Fons (1993) *Riding the Waves of Culture*, London: Nicholas Brealey.

Weinshall, Theodore (1977) *Culture and Management*, Harmondsworth: Penguin.

Whyte, W. F. (1955) *Organisation Man*, Harmondsworth: Penguin.

CHAPTER 11

European management

In the Todd Mall in Alice Springs in the middle of Australia (the mall is affectionately named after the chap who masterminded the overland telegraph, the town is named after his wife) there is one of those signposts that tells you the distance to faraway places. London is 15030 kilometres (9018 miles) away; Berlin, which lies in more or less the same direction, is a bit less far away, but not that much, so they seem to be close to each other. In other words, the closeness of two places depends on how far away from them you are. The same might be said of European management. In the previous chapter we detailed, even celebrated its heterogeneity. Yet if one adopts a suitably distant standpoint one might be rewarded with a homogeneous blur. So if one should ask whether there is any sense in which we can meaningfully speak of a European style of management, it is possible to answer yes – in spite of the differences paraded in the last chapter – if one compares Europe with some other substantial socioeconomic entity. Consider in this connection a possible comparison between Europe and Japan or the USA.

Europe versus Japan

Compared with Japan, management in Europe is more individualist. In Europe the focus is more on the needs of companies and people than on the needs of the country. Unlike the Japanese, Europeans are not given to stoicism or suppressing their individuality; they are therefore able to articulate their wants, needs and dissatisfactions. What is more these characteristics inform industrial relations in European countries and are part of the *raison d'être* of the industrial democracy or codetermination systems in some of these countries.

In Europe the purpose of business is to enhance the wealth of corporations rather than the grandeur of state. European corporations are distinct and identifiable, from each other and from society. In turn trade unions are distinct from corporations and are based on an aggregation of individual interests, not on a natural collectivism or fusion of beings. Management in Europe is about the acts and decisions of interacting individuals, it is not a set of collectivist processes.

In short one may contrast the individualism, separatism and articulation of Europe with the collectivism, processualism and inherence of Japan.

Europe versus the USA

European companies are more conservative than American ones. European companies are not as manifestly proactive, not as 'go-getting', not as exclusively concerned with results and performance. European companies tend to have longer time horizons than American ones: on average they are less short-termist, they report results less frequently and the impact of this reporting is typically weaker. There is no European equivalent to the phrase 'don't give me two bad quarters' (two successive three-month periods in which profitability declines).

European managers have more complex and more variable attitudes towards change and organisational conflict. Indeed where Americans see simple relationships between means and ends, Europeans see more complicated relationships. Americans believe that anything can be changed; Europeans are more wary, more sceptical regarding change. Americans know that everything is capable of being achieved – it is simply a matter of setting targets and allocating resources. Here too Europeans are more wary; some things seem to them inherently undoable, or if they can be done they are not worth the price in terms of disturbed relations. Where Americans see simple cause and effect, Europeans see conditionality and interplay of forces.

In the American scheme of things there is a rather narrow interpretation of what a given role requires, such that different incumbents of the same position tend to be rather alike. For example every politician is expected to be a glad-handing extrovert. Every manager is expected to be a proactive, systems-driven achiever. In Europe there is more tolerance of eccentricity, idiosyncrasy, difference and ambiguity. We Europeans do not expect our politicians, our executives, our high school students, even our aspirants for management traineeships to conform to a set of prescribed attributes and behaviours. It is instinctively understood in Europe that there is more than one way to skin a cat.

When it comes to management behaviour it is also understood in Europe that personality and style, background, social integration and interpersonal acceptance may impinge on selection for management posts and on the deportment of practising managers. In some European countries one must also take into account an element of deference. In the UK, for example, performance considerations will sometimes be modified by questions of 'fitting in'. Achievement may be judged in a context of relationships.

There is also a tendency among Europeans to think in terms of human qualities rather than American-inspired 'people skills'. The notion of human qualities implies more variation in personality type and style. Also implied is a less single-minded orientation.

European companies are more likely to recognise purposes and obligations that go beyond simple profitability, even if the provision of dividends to shareholders is the paramount objective. Such alternative considerations might include:

- Diffuse social obligations that relate to the cultural expectations of the organisation.
- The role of the company as employer.
- The role of the company as a local or regional institution.
- The role of the company as a focus of public esteem and affection (for example Marks & Spencer in the UK).
- The role of the company as a national emblem or torch bearer (examples include national carrier airlines such as Air France and Swissair).
- The role of the company as an instrument of government policy.

It is not suggested that these considerations are always present in Europe, still less that they will displace profitability goals, but simply that they are more likely to be present – to be part of the equation – in Europe than in the USA.

While both Europe and the USA are individualist rather than collectivist in Hofstede's terms (Hofstede, 1980), there is a difference of degree between them. In Europe individualism is not so pronounced, so unequivocal. Or to put it another way, European society takes a more conditional view of the rights of the individual. Freedom and choice are values in Europe, but they are not always supreme values. Community may limit choice, tradition may qualify freedom.

One small reflection of this is the attitude towards language. The American view of language is utilitarian, language is necessary as a means of expression, but no more than that. The individual's will and purposes dominate the mere currency of communication. Europeans tend to be more respectful of language, it is a cultural heritage rather than a tool. Style, resonance and allusion count as much as adequacy.

Mobility is another manifestation of this more qualified understanding of individualism in the European case. In the USA individualism and mobility are inseparable. It is, after all, the individual who is mobile – geographically, socially, occupationally – and this mobility expresses the individual's use of

freedom and the accomplishments it may bring. In particular mobility between employing organisations, intercompany mobility, expresses in the
American context an individual's drive, ambition and progress. But within
Europe attitudes towards intercompany mobility are more varied, more conditional. On the whole it is esteemed in Britain, but on somewhat different
grounds – that it will foster the development of judgement through wider
experience and contribute to an objective generalism. In France there is little
mobility, except at the top; in Germany any intercompany mobility is limited
to the confines of a given industry; in the Netherlands intercompany mobility
is regarded very negatively, as an expression of overweening ambition (how
un-American can you get!)

Companies in Europe accept more readily the existence of other institutions
that may impinge on their freedom and activities, for example European
corporations acknowledge, albeit sometimes grudgingly, the authority of the
state, the intervention of government. It is not that this does not happen in
the USA, but rather that the mythology proclaims all government to be bad
government. European companies are more tolerant, and may well perceive
advantage in 'talking to' government, indeed in a country such as Sweden an
ongoing dialogue with government seems perfectly natural, part of the executive role. What is more a number of the European countries have substantial
state-owned sectors – for instance Italy with its IRI and Spain with its INI –
both government holding companies – even if privatisation has been an inter-
mittent policy during the 1980s and 1990s.

But this European acceptance of other institutions is not limited to the state.
European businesses more readily accept trade unions, and in some countries
institutions of industrial democracy such as works councils and worker directors, or trade union directors or boards. Even in the depths of the manageralist
1990s, European companies have seldom sought to do more than reshape the
union–company relationship and alter the balance of power in favour of the
company. In Europe it is not an article of faith, as it is in the USA, that trade
unions represent an insupportable infraction of the managerial prerogative.
Europe also differs from the USA in recognising that there may well be an
ideological element in unionism – that union membership may in part derive
from class consciousness, may draw on a tradition of working-class solidarity,
may support reforms that go beyond the immediate interests of their members, may be linked to social-democratic political parties. Furthermore
European companies are more accepting of negotiation and compromise in
industrial relations, are less likely than their American counterparts to see
such exchanges in 'play to win', 'zero sum game' terms.

The more conditional view of individuality that prevails in Europe is also
reflected in the matter of performance appraisal. Performance appraisal, as
well as remuneration linked to performance appraisal, came from America to
Europe, and its reception has been variable to say the least. Appraisal in
Europe, especially the appraisal of senior personnel, differs from the

American norm in being less 'cut and dried', rather more creative, recognising the importance of intangible elements that defy codification. Appraisal in Europe is also more obviously contextualised by relationship considerations. In Europe pleasing people matters as well as achieving targets.

An integrating Europe?

Another possible approach to the issue of whether or not Europe is a meaningful entity is to ask whether there is any sense in which Europe is integrating, is coming together. Certainly if one considers the broad sweep of the twentieth century there is reason to suggest that it is.

First of all there has been no war in Western Europe since 1945. And in the aftermath of the Second World War those historic enemies, France and Germany, were reconciled. This fact is now so absolutely taken for granted that it is difficult to appreciate what a remarkable development it was – politically, diplomatically and economically. Just consider how impossible such a reconciliation would have been at the end of the First World War (1914–18) and how much suffering the world would have been spared if those two states had been reconciled at that time.

Indeed even in Eastern Europe there were not really any wars until 1991 and the break-up of the former USSR and Yugoslavia, although during the communist period military force was used to quell opposition to the regime, and this sometimes happened cross-border, as in the Russian intervention in Hungary in 1956 and in Czechoslovakia in 1968. A significant element of Europeans' shock and horror at the civil war in Yugoslavia and the fighting in various parts of the former USSR in the 1990s was precisely the fact that war on the European continent had become unthinkable.

Continuing this macro-theme of the pacification and integration of Europe during the course of the twentieth century, the collapse of European communism in the 1989–91 period marked the end of a major divide, dramatically symbolised by the reunification of Germany in 1990. As previous chapters have stressed, the countries of post-communist Eastern Europe are still very different from those of Western Europe, but they *want* to be like Western Europe – democratic, capitalist and affluent.

At a more modest level, post-1945 Western Europe spawned a number of superanational organisations: the OECD, the Benelux Union, the Nordic Union, the European Defence Community, and above all, of course, the EEC/EC/EU from 1958.

The EU has been the integrating force *par excellence*. In the first decade of its life it was dominated by the newly reconciled France and Germany, but it grew steadily. The original group of six member states was enlarged by the accession of Britain, Denmark and the Republic of Ireland in 1973; then Greece joined, followed by Spain and Portugal. Then there was the watershed of the Single European Market in 1992, discussed in Chapter 2. In 1995 three more states joined (Sweden, Finland and Austria), swelling the number of member countries to fifteen. In Western Europe only Norway and Switzerland are not members, the Norwegian citizens having voted twice to revoke Norway's application to join. As the century draws to a close a host of post-communist East European states are clamouring to join.

One of the EU's programmes has also had a quietly integrating effect at the human rather than the regulatory level, and this is the Erasmus (now Socrates) student exchange scheme. As a consequence of these programmes a growing proportion of young people are receiving part of their higher education in an institution in another EU member state. And it is surprising how one has come to take it all for granted, that there will always be subgroups of French, Spanish and German students in one's lectures, that all colleges will have their network of Erasmus partners, that joint (two-institution, two-country) degree schemes have flourished since the mid 1980s.

Finally in this *tour d'horizon* of integrating forces it is worth remarking that Europe, meaning primarily the EU, is increasingly seen as a single entity by outsiders. This was very clear in the run-up to the Single European Market, when the phrase 'fortress Europe' was coined to describe the presumed exclusivity and impregnability of the EU bloc (never mind that this was wrong, that the SEM was only about non-tariff barriers, that no exclusion was intended). Indeed in this run-up period there was a scramble among Japanese, American and even Australian firms to 'get in' before it was too late – a testimony to the power of conviction rather than reality. A nicely observed and authentic formulation of this Europe-as-a-perceived-entity view is that of the influential American economist Lester Thurow in his book *Head to Head* (1992). Writing in the early 1990s Thurow argued that Europe at that time was in the position enjoyed by the USA at the end of the Second World War. Europe (principally the EU no doubt) was dominant, the largest market, and would therefore 'write the terms of trade' as the USA did at the Bretton Woods conference in 1944. The twenty-first century, asserted Thurow, should be Europe's century, as the twentieth century was America's. The EU would get bigger, the Eastern European countries would have to be admitted (in Thurow's view because otherwise they would constitute a disorderly mess on West Europe's eastern border), and to protect and privilege Eastern Europe the EU would economically deprivilege the rest of the world, including the USA.

Admittedly Thurow's position is an extreme one. It is also conceivable that given the chance Thurow might modify the views he expressed in 1992 in the light of the development of the USA-led NAFTA trading bloc on one side of the Atlantic and the problems of achieving monetary union in the EU on the other side. Nonetheless Thurow's view is interesting as a non-European perspective on Europe. It is the Alice Springs phenomenon again: if one looks at

Europe from a distance, in this case from Cambridge Massachusetts, a unitary entity may be perceived.

Diversity as defining feature

Another way to approach the issue of Europe is to accept that the region displays a high level of diversity, and then to view that diversity as an essential characteristic of the region. Consider the following:

- Europe embraces a large number of independent nation states in relation to its geographic area (18 in Western Europe alone, without counting Liechtenstein and Andorra).
- In Western Europe all of these states have been independent throughout the twentieth century, and in many cases – Spain, France, Switzerland, Britain – for hundreds of years.
- This in turn implies lots of separate nation-state-embedded institutions, as argued in the previous chapter using the LEST research to illustrate the point.
- The same limited geographic area boasts a large number of languages, and only in the case of the three Scandinavian languages is there a similarity between them.

The four claims articulated above could not be made for North America, Latin America, the Middle East, Sub-Saharan Africa or Australasia. Europe offers diversity crossed with durability.

The management of diversity

This in turn raises the question: if diversity is a differentiating feature of Europe, are European companies good at *managing* diversity? This is of course an entirely valid question, even though it is difficult to envisage the sort of data that might be needed to provide a definitive answer. Still, a few reflections may be in order.

First of all it is noteworthy that European countries have a very positive attitude towards exporting, which in turn implies the need to address the question of the (potentially) different demands and contingencies of the countries exported to. This positive attitude towards exporting characterises both the large and the small countries of Europe – Europe includes the world's largest exporting country (Germany) and the country that exports the largest proportion of GDP (the Netherlands). A comparison with the USA is particularly instructive in this matter.

For the typical American company the American market is more important (more substantial and more valuable) than any other market. Export or die has never been an American shibboleth. This attitude is accentuated by the American tendency to service other markets, especially European ones, by means of manufacturing subsidiaries rather than by direct exports. This can in part be explained by geography, in the sense that the distance between the USA and Europe is greater than that between Britain and France, but it is also in part a matter of mindset. Referring back to the discussion of the brewing industry in Chapter 3, consider for example that Heineken services the US market by shipping beer brewed in Amsterdam, but Anheuser Busch services the European market by means of licensing agreements. Or referring back to Chapter 5 it is interesting that Bartlett and Ghoshall (1989) suggest that European multinational companies general as tend towards a multidomestic orientation, that is, they tend to differentiate products and services according to receiving markets and to be structured accordingly.

Second, in Europe a number of companies are jointly owned by the governments of or shareholders in two or more countries. The Scandinavian airline SAS is quite unique in being owned by three governments, or as the Norwegian joke has it; 'SAS is run by Swedes, for the benefit of Danes, and paid for by the Norwegians'. There is also ABB (Asea Brown Boverie), a joint Swedish–Swiss company that is headquartered in Zürich and has a Swedish chief executive. In the Netherlands two of the top three companies, Shell and Unilever, are not exclusively Dutch but Anglo-Dutch, with headquarters in both countries. And of course Airbus is a multinational cooperation.

Third, throughout the 1980s and 1990s Europe has witnessed a range of cross-border mergers and acquisitions. In Chapter 3 on the brewing industry we drew attention to the fact that most breweries in Spain and Italy are foreign owned (principally by other Europeans), or at least breweries based in other countries have ownership stakes in Spanish and Italian breweries. But this phenomenon is not of course limited to brewing. In the car industry Volkswagen of Germany acquired SEAT of Spain in 1986; in confectionery Nestlé of Switzerland acquired Rowntree of Britain in 1988; in drinks Pedro Domecq of Spain and Allied Lyons of Britain merged; in 'white goods' Electrolux of Sweden acquired Zanussi of Italy, and so it goes on.

Europe has also been open to cross-border strategic alliances. To take just one industry, banking, unpublished research by ul-Haq in 1996 has revealed a myriad of cross-border strategic alliances in European banking, mostly in order to share risks and costs, or to acquire access for particular products to another national market. Banking also offers examples of cross-border strategic alliances of a broader kind, where the contracting partners have come together to pool resources and formulate objectives on a wider front; examples here would be the alliance between the Banco de Santander of Spain and the Royal Bank of Scotland, and that between France's BNP and Germany's Dresdener Bank.

None of this, of course, constitutes conclusive evidence of a European capability to manage diversity, but these sets of examples suggest a disposition that is at least favourable to diversity rather than American-style domination through standardisation (Lawrence, 1996).

We shall end this discussion of the management of diversity by looking at a company in an industry we have used several times for illustrative purposes in this book. The industry is chocolate and confectionery, the company is Nestlé.

Nestlé's principal R&D centre for chocolate and biscuits is situated on the site of the Rowntree factory in York, England (not in Nestlé's home country Switzerland, although there is a central R&D centre in Lausanne near the Vevey headquarters). What is interesting about the York R&D centre in the present context is that it is avowedly multinational and multicultural, that is, the researchers are neither exclusively English nor primarily English, but are drawn from a variety of countries in which Nestlé operates. Europeans predominate – British, French, Swiss, Dutch, German and Italian – but there are also representatives of the New World and Australia. This did not come about by accident: the operating rule is that no more than 25 per cent of the research staff at the York centre should be British.

The declared reasons for this state of affairs are also interesting. Paramount is the conviction that the development of consumer products destined for a variety of mostly rather sophisticated markets cannot be entrusted to the representatives of just one national market, whatever specialisms or expertise the country concerned might possess. Second, it is agreed that the different nationals will be reciprocally stimulating, will spark off each other, will make for greater creativity. One example of this 'sparking off' is the meeting of French strength in formal reasoning with pragmatic British lateral thinking.

There is more to come. Part of the case for the belief that European companies and their managers are good at the management of diversity is predicated on a challenge and response hypothesis. That is to say, Europeans are more diverse than anyone else, *ipso facto* they must have addressed the management of diversity and got better at it than non-Europeans. Perfectly rational, but not conclusive of course. Now consider a variation on this theme of challenge and response, the integration of R&D into the company.

The integration of R&D is typically problematic in the world of manufacturing. R&D staff are marked off by superior education, they may be quasi-academics rather than career managers, their commitment may be to a research specialism rather than to industry or a particular company, and so. It is even often the case that R&D is physically separate from manufacturing in the sense that production takes place in a noisy factory while R&D is located in a converted chateau outside Grenoble or a country house in the Thames Valley.

The challenge to integrate R&D is nowhere greater than in a consumer products company in a multidomestic industry, headquartered in one small European country but with most of the operations and the generation of revenue occurring in other larger countries. Nestlé have in part solved the problem of integration by adopting the multicultural stance discussed above, but there are other specifics.

First, the R&D centre is located on a major manufacturing site, as noted. Second, some of the researchers are seconded from companies in a variety of countries and will probably return to them, which is an integrating force. Third, while the majority of specialist researchers are directly recruited from universities, in a number of countries, they are also picked for their management potential, so that they can move through R&D and out into line management positions. Fourth, even the few who have long-term R&D career aspirations, who see themselves as eventually becoming senior R&D managers, will make repeated moves between research and operations on the way up. It is a nice instance of the parallel management of diversity, in this case diversity of corporate functions.

European managers: a common view

Insofar as one can point to a European management style, in however qualified a fashion, it is fair to ask: does European management have a common view? The bulk of the available evidence suggests that it does not. From Hofstede's 1970s data on employee values and choices (Hofstede, 1980) to the Nene study of the late 1990s, the suggestion is that groups of managers from different (European) countries will articulate different views of authority, change, conflict, cooperation, the determinants of corporate success and so on, and up-to-date illustrations of this propensity were given in the previous chapter.

One can, however, take the views of managers from a number of European countries and aggregate them in the sense of working out a pan-European score for their responses to different questionnaire items, and we did this with the Nene study. Not too much should be made of this study in the sense that while the sample size was reasonable (managers from Sweden, Holland, Germany, Italy, and Britain) it did not include a French or Spanish sample. Nonetheless it will be quite entertaining to aggregate the scores and see what these European managers, forcibly collectivised, agreed upon.

The survey took the form of a battery of propositions to which the managers responded on a scale from strongly agree to strongly disagree. Most of the propositions were formulated in a positive manner, so there were few 'strongly disagree' responses and the bulk of the responses ranged from neutral or mildly agree to strongly agree. The score was one for strongly agree and five for strongly disagree, and one can identify a small number of questionnaire items where the mean score was between one and two; that is, the propositions that were most strongly affirmed and the ones upon which there was most cross-country agreement. The result of the exercise is really quite instructive.

First, there was a positive view on environmental matters. The proposition 'Business should be made to pay for environmental damage resulting from their production process and the use of their products' attracted a mean score of 1.76. A proposition to the effect that environmentally friendly products are sometimes perceived as ineffective was rejected; and so, in the same context, was the proposition that a company's exclusive responsibility is to its shareholders. At the same time the environment was seen as presenting business opportunities: the proposition 'Engineering environmentally friendly products opens up a new source of competitive advantage for companies' received a mean score of 1.95.

There was a recognition of the rights of individuals within companies to voice their views and to appeal to senior people. The propositions 'Everyone, whatever their status, should have the right to say what they think' and 'An employee should feel able to make contact with the head of their organisation if they wish' both had mean scores of between one and two, as did a proposition extolling semi-autonomous team working.

But the dominating theme in terms of propositions strongly affirmed across the European countries was that of change. Of the 72 propositions, the one that received the highest mean score was 'Change affects all people in an organisation: managers, therefore, need to consult widely to facilitate the implementation of change.' In second place was 'Change is normal in business life and management work', and also strongly affirmed was the proposition 'The rate of change in business life in the present decade [the 1990s] is greater than ever before.'

Another of the propositions sought to determine what might be comprehended by the word 'change', *viz*. 'Business is changing now in the sense of a radical questioning of all the old arrangements: so, for example, separate industries are collapsed into each other, product market segments are defined in new ways, competitive advantage is differently construed, and so on.' This was strongly affirmed. Interestingly not only did the German managers, who tend to be the least strategically aware, buy this proposition, they affirmed it more strongly than the participants from the other European countries (a greater innocence to lose, perhaps).

On the same theme, propositions to the effect that (1) employees must expect change, (2) career development is less predictable and (3) concern for job security is growing, all showed European mean scores of between one and two. Side by side with this dominant theme of the awareness of far-reaching change was a sense of heightened competition. The proposition 'Companies today can no longer have success primarily on product quality; the need is rather to exploit a variety of other competitive advantages' received a mean score of 1.74 (again with the Germans, perhaps surprisingly, scoring higher). A related proposition that companies must take account of the actions of competitors in other countries, and preempt them, received a European mean score of 1.66, and the proposition 'No market is secure, no business segment is discrete, no company is safe from take-over: this is the essence of today's business world' a mean score of 1.65. Perhaps this says it all.

Europe in Focus

This book has been about the tension between Europe's inherited diversity and homogenising forces. Having explored a number of dimensions that impinge on this issue, were we to ask the question 'Is Europe more homogeneous at the end of the twentieth century than it was at the middle of that century?' what would be the answer?

The easiest reply would be that the question is unanswerable. It is not a simple question, even though it is simply formulated. There are a number of major strands running through the issue of diversity–homogeneity and an investigation of these different strands may yield different answers, and when one tries to put them together one finds a complex of conflicting forces and integrating trends. Yet it may still be helpful to disaggregate the problem, break it down into a manageable number of strands and see where each of these takes us.

We suggest that there are four key dimensions, none of which are simple in their substance or effect.

Geopolitical

First of all there are a number of geopolitical considerations, which have been briefly reviewed earlier in the present chapter. These include the absence of war in Western Europe for half a century, the reconciliation of France and Germany, the postwar solidarity of Western Europe under American leadership and in response to a perceived communist threat, the unprecedented expansion in world trade and economic development after the Second World War, and the corresponding growth in disposable income that has benefited most of the populations of Western Europe. All this seems to make the difference between being Belgian or Swiss, Dutch or Austrian rather less meaningful than it was in the first half of the century and before.

Then a decade before the end of the century we witnessed the collapse of European communism. This served to reinforce the trend towards homogeneity: at a stroke a political threat, a rival ideology and an alternative economic system were removed, providing a great boost to European unity. In less than a year after the opening of the Berlin Wall Germany was reunited, something that had seemed utterly improbable five years earlier. And as the century draws to a close these former communist states are being admitted to NATO and clamouring to enter the EU.

There is however, a sting in the tale of the collapse of European communism. Throughout the communist period the armed might of the communist states had suppressed ethnicity within their borders. When this central power collapsed, old ethnic differences resurfaced and became a problem in all the post-communist states. Three of them – Czechoslovakia, Yugoslavia and the USSR – actually fell apart.

At a more subtle level the collapse of communism revealed the extent of heterogeneity in Central and Eastern Europe. As we have seen in earlier chapters, the differences between the countries, which had been masked by the stranglehold of communism, reemerged: the West discovered that they had done different things under communism, racked up different levels of foreign debt, developed the non-state sector to different degrees and so on. The approaches taken by the post-communist states in the transition to capitalism have also varied: they have adopted different approaches to the privatisation of state-owned enterprises, attracted different amounts of foreign direct investment from the West, and so on. It may be that in the medium term the collapse of European communism will lead to greater homogeneity, but this is not a foregone conclusion.

The European Union

The EU is undoubtedly a force for homogenisation. Since its inception in 1958 its influence has grown in three ways:

- Founded as a tariff union, through the 1992–93 Single European Market initiative (discussed in Chapter 2) it moved to eliminate non-tariff barriers as well in a bid to make the union more effective, more like a United States of Europe.
- It has progressively extended the range of things it seeks to regulate, control and harmonise, to the point where monetary union is a firm objective and political union is waiting in the wings.
- It has grown much larger: between 1958 and 1995 the number of member states rose from six to 15, further enlargement is expected, and the two Western European countries – Norway and Switzerland – that have stood out against (full) membership are increasingly affected by it.

Yet the homogenising influence of the EU is far from total. It has striven for administrative, regulatory and now fiscal harmonisation of its member states. However it has not addressed the question of socio-cultural diversity, and its impact on national institutions of education, training and industrial relations has been modest.

Business trends

Business trends are probably the most powerful and pervasive force for homogeneity, yet these trends are difficult to apprehend, and they can never be quite determining in their effect on individual companies.

First of all it is clear that some trends, as explained in Chapter 2, are cross-border anyway, and have merely been accentuated by the Single European Market initiative. For instance developments such as concentration, bipolarisation, segmentation and so on have been recognised as persistent trends throughout the 1980s and 1990s.

Second, if one takes particular industries and examines their operations in a variety of European countries, as we did in Chapter 4, again a number of similarities emerge. They segment their product markets in broadly similar ways, are subject to the same industry-wide developments, have the same concerns, identify the same issues and have broadly similar strategic perceptions.

But again this is not the whole story. If one looks at a particular industry and takes as a starting point its presence in various European countries, as we did with the brewing industry in Chapter 3, then a whole range of differences emerge. Variations in national tastes impact on the demand for the industry's products, it is differently organised in the various countries, has a different place in their national economies, its representative companies achieve different degrees of dominance in world markets, and different configurations of cross-border ownership and operation develop.

It is possible to categorise industries in global, international and multidomestic terms, to specify their strategic rationale and indeed their key operational features. Yet as we have seen in Chapter 5, reality is not as neat as theory. Many of these industries turn out to be 'mixed', giving pride of place neither to global integration nor to local adaptation exigencies, but doing different things in different circumstances. And while one can identify the principal determinants of strategy, these are not absolute in their effect. While many may conform, some will reconfigure their capabilities and act in ways that are not programmable. So business trends and strategic rationality are forces for homogenisation, but they do not always have predictable outcomes. We should beware of an overdetermined view of the conduct of companies.

Management style and behaviour

Finally there is the issue of management values, style and practice, and the variations between countries are well-documented. To repeat an argument from the previous chapter, these differences not only reflect the socio-cultural heritage and conditioning that goes with being a citizen of one country rather than another, it is also the case that these countries, independent nation states, have developed a variety of institutions and systems – of education, industrial relations, vocational training and so on – that also help to structure the world of (management) work. And as far as we can judge from the cross-cultural and comparative management literature, these differences have been remarkably stable over the last 30–40 years. The Nene study, discussed above, showed that managers from several European countries are united in their horror at the *rate* of change, but relatively little else. There may be a clue to the future in this last finding.

There is a tendency in discussions of country-based management differences to assume that while differences count at the moment, they will tend to get less and less over time. If made explicit, the idea of diminishing difference is couched in terms of the growth of international encounter (more people from all countries meeting more people from other countries than ever before). But this formulation is probably questionable. Simply meeting people who exhibit differences from oneself, foreigners in this case, is not likely to reduce those differences. Indeed it may reinforce them, with one group redefining its national identity by encountering its opposite. International encounter has been increasing steadily, in and out of business, for half a century, without apparently eroding the differences between, say, French and German managers.

On the other hand there may be some other elements of international business, not simple human contact, that do help dissolve national differences. The most likely candidate here is fierceness of competition, which is being enhanced by the internationalisation of markets and operations, and managerial perceptions stemming from this are clearly identifiable in some of the Nene survey responses cited earlier in this chapter.

The issue might be formulated in a different way. In the last twenty years or so of the twentieth century the Anglo-Saxon model of capitalism – aggressive, competitive, proactive, shareholder driven and strategically aware – seems to have become more dominant. Manifestations such as merger and acquisition activity, cross-border initiatives, strategic sorties and retaliations have become more pronounced in the USA and certainly in the UK, and have also begun to make their appearance in other countries where business has been rather differently construed in the past. Within the EU, France is a case in point: during the 1990s France has seen liberalisation/deregulation, privatisation and an internationalisation that goes beyond Europeanisation, together with the rise of a new ethical accountability, with chief executives being proceeded against for corruption and other wrongdoings. Such developments have been accentuated by the growing regulatory might of the EU, especially since the advent of the Single European Market, which is tending to restrict the role of the French state in business. These moves, together with mild managerial unemployment in France, may serve to undermine or even transform the étatist, bureaucratic, formalistic, educationally elitist model of French management.

It should be emphasised that this argument is no more than speculative. But it is possible that change in the business system may impact on management values and practice, and this is nowhere more likely than in the EU.

References

Bartlett, C. A. and S. Ghoshal (1989) *Managing Across Borders*, London: Hutchinson.
Hofstede, Geert (1980) *Culture's Consequence*, Beverly Hills, LA: Sage.
Lawrence, Peter (1996) *Management in the USA*, London: Sage.
Thurow, Lester (1992) *Head to Head*, New York: William Morrow.

*Index**

* Compiled by Meg Davies (Registered Indexer, Society of Indexers).